# 英语写作教程：以内容为依托
## Content-based English Writing
## （下册）

邹涛　张杨　主编

**图书在版编目(CIP)数据**

英语写作教程：以内容为依托(下册)/邹涛，张杨主编.—北京：北京大学出版社，2013.1
(21世纪英语专业系列教材)
ISBN 978-7-301-21570-8

Ⅰ.①英… Ⅱ.①邹…②张… Ⅲ.①英语－写作－高等学校－教材 Ⅳ.①H315

中国版本图书馆CIP数据核字(2012)第270177号

书　　　　名：英语写作教程：以内容为依托(下册)
著作责任者：邹　涛　张　杨　主编
责　任　编　辑：孙　莹
标　准　书　号：ISBN 978-7-301-21570-8/H·3178
出　版　发　行：北京大学出版社
地　　　　址：北京市海淀区成府路205号　100871
网　　　　址：http://www.pup.cn　新浪官方微博：@北京大学出版社
电　子　信　箱：zbing@pup.pku.edu.cn
电　　　　话：邮购部 62752015　发行部 62750672　编辑部 62754382　出版部 62754962
印　刷　者：北京中科印刷有限公司
经　销　者：新华书店
　　　　　　787毫米×1092毫米　16开本　10印张　280千字
　　　　　　2013年1月第1版　2014年1月第2次印刷
定　　　价：26.00元

未经许可，不得以任何方式复制或抄袭本书之部分或全部内容。
版权所有，侵权必究
举报电话：010-62752024　电子信箱：fd@pup.pku.edu.cn

本教材是"985工程"之"优秀教学团队支持计划"——"英语写作教学团队"(项目编号为 A1098521-029)以及全国教育科学"十二五"规划 2011 年度教育部重点课题"高校公共英语写作系列课程设计与教学方法研究"(项目编号为 GPA115005)的阶段性成果。

*Reading makes a full man; conference a ready man; and writing an exact man.*
—Francis Bacon

读书使人充实,讨论使人机敏,写作使人严谨。
——培根

# 编委会名单

**全书总主编** 邹　涛　张　杨
**上册副主编** 王琪欣　吕　汀　袁毅敏
**下册副主编** 邢　青　肖飞燕　龙　梅

# 序　言

在我国，随着哑巴式英语学习的困境逐渐解除，写作环节的问题日益凸显。学生在写作中要么无话可写，要么有话表达不好。那一份份内容空洞、错误频出的英语毕业论文，也许是对写作问题的最好见证。写作老师们变得无所适从，当他们耐心地从词句段篇按步骤分学期讲解时，学生因早早面对各种英语考试中的写作而心急如焚；当部分老师痛下决心扔掉国内教材而与国际接轨时，又发现英文原版教材的很多话题存在明显的水土不服问题。市面上针对考试或特殊用途的写作教材数量繁多，却并不适于基础阶段的写作教学。基于以上困境，本书编委在写作教学改革与实践基础上，试图结合中西写作教材的优势，以编写新教材为牵引带动写作教学模式的革新。

本书编写理念为以内容为依托的教学法（content-based instruction，简称CBI）。不过，这里的"内容"不是某个专门的学科知识，而是适应于基础写作教学需求、让学生感觉亲切而有表达兴趣的话题。CBI教学法在本教材中体现在以下三个方面：

其一，本教材摈弃以写作技巧为纲的传统编写模式，而是通过广泛的问卷调查，选取与学生学习生活密切相关的十大话题为编写框架，以尽可能激起学生讨论和写作的兴趣，让其产生表达的冲动和欲望；

其二，每章精选三篇范文，在文章内容及问题设计上尽可能体现跨文化视野（注意中西文化差异对比）和时代意识（注意传统与当下的对比），兼顾范文的语言质量（语言地道）与思想高度（富有启发性），以便真正激发学生的讨论兴趣并便于写作模仿。

其三，我们在每一章的写作任务设计时紧紧围绕某个具体话题，从词、句、段、章各个层面紧扣该话题进行引导，努力让课文最后的篇章写作任务水到渠成。

其四，为帮助学生掌握每个话题的核心关键词的地道搭配，编委成员自创大学英语语料库，收录目前市面上广泛使用的十余套大学英语教材以及本套教材的选文，通过语料库检索，引导学生对每章话题的关键词进行地道的语言搭配训练。

为解决因以话题为纲而可能带来的技巧训练不成体系这一问题，我们采用了两种策略：

其一，我们在开篇的Introduction部分对写作过程和写作策略进行了整体性的介绍，帮助学生对写作形成一个整体概观。

其二，我们将Introduction中提到的各个层面（词、句、段、章）的写作技巧看作Basic Writing Techniques，以其为线索进行练习设计，将这些技巧在每一章的具体文本中进行阐释、演绎和模仿，使学生在不断的强化中真正领会基本写作技巧的具体应用。所以，请读者不要因每篇出现的技巧分析而厌倦。万变不离其宗，只要你真正学会了从这些角度去思考任何一篇文章，你的阅读和写作能力也水到渠成。

练习设计的具体思路如下：我们强调对学生的批判思维的训练，第一部分Critical reader重在引导学生把握文章主旨并进行思维拓展，努力让学生有话可说、想说。其中的Critical reader A 主要提醒学生阅读过程中需要注意的问题；Critical reader B 主要针对读完全文后的思维拓展。第二部分Critical writer重在引导学生理解和掌握思想呈现、表达的方式，让学生有话能说。其中Basic Writing Techniques这部分以Introduction中提到的各个层面的写作技巧为线索，将这些技巧一一运用到每个具体文本中；Specific Writing Techniques这部分针对Basic Writing Techniques练习中未涵盖的其他写作技巧进行阐释和演练。最后以篇章写作任务收尾。

附录一收录了应用文写作范例，为学生的日常英语写作提供帮助；附录二整理出英式英语与美式英语对照简表。负责审校本教材英语部分的美国外教Frederic Cubbage指出，中国学生在口语上学的大都是美式英语，而他们阅读的教材内容却英式美式混杂，导致他们的英语语言输出也是混杂状态，让地道的美国人或英国人感觉很别扭，甚至常常产生误解。他的意见引起我们的反思，意识到中国老师和学生在教与学的过程中确实很容易忽视英式英语与美式英语的差异。有鉴于此，我们制定了附录二，虽然受篇幅所限收录的内容不多，但旨在提醒学生在英语表达过程中注意针对不同的对象而有所选择。

本教材主要供英语专业基础写作课以及非英语专业的优生班英语写作课使用。在进入具体的章节之前，强烈建议读者先认真读完导论，以快速形成一个有关写作的整体认识，这样能很好地理解后面十章和Introduction部分的呼应关系。在话题排序上，我们根据问卷调查结果，按照话题和学生心理距离远近、熟悉程度高低降序排列。但是，有些话题之间的差距并不明显，所以，教师或自学者可以根据实际需求选择话题顺序。此外，因为每一章都包括了词、句、段、章各层的写作训练，各章自成一个相对完整的写作训练体系，也加大了使用的灵活性。

本教材编写过程历经两年半。在写作教学改革项目的推动下，我们对编写内容反复思考、讨论、修订和检验，最终形成此稿。不当之处，恳请方家读者指正，以便进一步完善。

本教材编委按章节顺序具体分工如下：邹涛编写导论、第一章，负责全书思路制定和全书审稿；吕汀编写第二章、附录二；袁毅敏编写第三章、参编第九章；王琪欣编写第四章、第五章；肖飞燕编写第六章、附录一；张杨编写第七章，负责提供语料库及使用技术，以及全书格式审校；龙梅编写第八章、主编第九章；邢青编写第十章，参与下册审稿；Frederic Cubbage负责全书英文审校。

邹涛

2012年7月于成都

# Contents

**Chapter Six  Health** ............................................................................................ 1
   Text A   The Solid Flesh ........................................................................... 1
   Text B   On Going to Bed ......................................................................... 14
   Text C   Agony From Ecstasy .................................................................. 21
   Corpus-based Exercises (6) ....................................................................... 25

**Chapter Seven  The Wonders of Nature** ............................................................ 30
   Text A   Nature ........................................................................................ 30
   Text B   A Short Look at the Colorful World of Flowers ........................ 39
   Text C   Unsolved Mystery—the Sea ....................................................... 44
   Corpus-based Exercises (7) ....................................................................... 48

**Chapter Eight  Entertainment** ............................................................................ 54
   Text A   Old Blue Eyes: A Look at the Life of Frank Sinatra .................. 54
   Text B   The Jordan Mystique .................................................................. 64
   Text C   Dressing as the Hillbilly Cat ....................................................... 70
   Corpus-based Exercises (8) ....................................................................... 73

**Chapter Nine  Future Plans** ................................................................................ 75
   Text A   Life after Graduation: To Work or Not to Work? ...................... 75
   Text B   Priority Setting—Why? .............................................................. 83
   Text C   Application Letter ...................................................................... 91
   Corpus-based Exercises (9) ....................................................................... 97

**Chapter Ten  Controversial Issues** .................................................................... 100
   Text A   Civilized Society Distorted by Moral Apathy ........................... 100
   Text B   Death and Justice ....................................................................... 110
   Text C   People Should Choose When to Retire ...................................... 123
   Corpus-based Exercises (10) ..................................................................... 129

**Appendix I  Practical Writing Samples** ........................................................... 132

**Appendix II  British English vs. American English** ........................................ 146

# Chapter Six

# Health

### Warming up

With the advancement of society, the prosperity of the economy and the fast-paced rhythm of the modern life style, physical well-being is becoming a great concern of people of all ages and all stations. Therefore, physical exercise is becoming widespread as a well-received concept, a popular fashion, and even an irresistible culture. What have you observed and witnessed regarding this fitness wave? Have you come in close contact with, or been involved in such a trend? What is your attitude toward this prevalent phenomenon?

## Text A

### The Solid Flesh

by Simeon Strunsky (1879—1948)

#### A Critical Reader (I)

1. What is the topic sentence of Paragraph 1?
2. What is the author's perspective on and attitude toward the physical culture?
3. What expressions could effectively convey the author's stance?
4. What kind of motions does Harrington make in his daily morning exercise?

1. Physical culture as pursued in the home probably benefits a man's body; but the strain on his moral nature is terrific. I go through my morning exercise with hatred for all the world and contempt for myself. Why, for instance, should every system of gymnastics require that a man place himself in the most ridiculous and unnatural postures? A stout, middle-aged man who struggles to touch the floor with the palms of his hands is not a beautiful sight. Equally preposterous¹ is the practice of standing on one leg and stretching the other toward the nape² of one's neck. In the confines of a city bedroom such evolutions are not only ungraceful but frequently dangerous.

2. Harrington tells me that every morning when he lunges³ forward he scrapes the tips of his fingers against the edge of the bed and the tears come into his eyes. When he throws his arms back he hits the gas jet. Harrington's young son, who insists on being present during the ordeal, believes that the entire performance is intended for his amusement, and laughs immoderately. I cannot blame him.

Morning exercise is incompatible with the maintenance of parental dignity. Were I a child again I could neither love nor respect a father who placed two chairs at a considerable distance from each other and mounted them horizontally like the human bridge in a melodrama[4].

3. I admit, of course, that home exercises have the merit of being cheap. No special apparatus is required. The ordinary household furniture and such heirlooms[5] are readily available will usually suffice. An onyx clock will do instead of chest weights. Any two volumes of the *Encyclopaedia Britannica* will take the place of dumb-bells or Indian clubs. Many a time I have stood still and held a bronze lamp in my outstretched right hand for a minute and then held it in my left hand for half a minute. I know of one man who skipped the rope one hundred times every morning. Within four months he had lost three and a half pounds, and driven the family in the flat below into nervous prostration. I have even been told that there are systems of exercise which show how physical perfection may be attained by scientifically manipulating, for fifteen minutes every day, a couple of fountain pens and a paper cutter. But I cannot reconcile myself to such methods because of the confusion they introduce into the world of common things. A table is no longer something to write upon or to eat upon, but something to lie down upon while one flings out his arms and legs fifty times in four contrary directions. A broom-stick is an instrument for strengthening the shoulder muscles. When I see a transom, I find myself estimating the number of times I could chin it.

4. The intimate connection between the hygienic life and the temptation to tell lies is a delicate subject to touch upon; but the facts may as well be brought out now as later. People of otherwise irreproachable conduct will lose all sense of truthfulness when they speak of physical culture and fresh air. They will exaggerate the number of inches they keep their bedroom windows raised in midwinter; they will quote ridiculous estimates of the doctors' bills they have saved; they will represent themselves as being in the most incredibly perfect health. I know one sober, intelligent business-man who not only habitually understates, by ten degrees, the temperature of his morning tub, but gives an altogether

[5] How is such a morning scene interpreted and understood in the eyes of Harrington's young son and in your eyes?

[6] What is the merit of home exercise? And how such an advantage is illustrated and exemplified in the following description?

[7] Does the author see eye to eye on such applauded benefit? If not, what is his counter-argument?

[8] What is the topic sentence of Paragraph 4?

[9] What kind of lies is a man tempted to tell when touching upon the topic of hygienic life?

[10] What kind of lies is a man tempted to tell when touching upon the topic of hygienic life?

[11] What is the main idea of Paragraph 5?

distorted impression of the alacrity with which he leaps into his bath every morning, and the reluctance with which he leaves it. This same man asserts that he can now walk from the Chambers Street ferry to his office in Wall Street in astonishing time. And not only that, but since he took to walking as much as he could, he has cut down his daily number of cigars to one-fourth (which is untrue). And not only that, but since he has gone in for exercise and fresh air and has given up smoking, his income has increased by at least 50 per cent, owing to his improved health and clearer mental vision. But that again, as I happen to know, is untrue.

5. But there is another, much more subtle form of prevarication[6]. Smith meets you in the street and remarks upon your flabby appearance. He argues that you ought to weigh twenty-five pounds less than you do, and that a long daily walk will do the trick. "Look at me," he says, "I walk ten miles every day and there isn't an ounce of superfluous[7] flesh on me." And so saying, he slaps his chest and offers to let you feel how hard the muscles are about his diaphragm[8]. Of course, there is no superfluous flesh on Smith. And if he abstained entirely from physical exertion and guzzled heavy German beer all day and dined on turtle soup and roast goose every day, and ate unlimited quantities of pastry, he would still be what he describes as free from superfluous flesh. I call it scraggy[9]. Smith is one of the men set apart by nature to perpetuate the Don Quixote[10] type of beauty, just as I am doomed with the lapse of time to approximate the Falstaffian[11] type. Smith's five sisters and brothers are thin. His father was slight and neurasthenic. His mother was spare and angular. Little wonder the Smith family is fond of walking. Friction and air-resistance in their case are practically nonexistent.

6. I do not, of course, mean to deny the ancient tradition that a sound body makes a sound mind. But I would only point out that we are just beginning to wake to the truth of the converse proposition, that a sane, equable, easy-going mind keeps the body well. Hence there are really two kinds of exercise, and two kinds of hygiene, a physical kind and a spiritual kind. Which one a man will choose should be left entirely to himself. It is only a question of approaching the same goal from two different

12 What expressions are the equivalents of the word "thin" in this paragraph?

13 What is the author's converse proposition? What is the relationship between the original proposition and this converse one?

14 What is your interpretation of "they tire out the soul in trying to serve it"?

15 What kind of malevolent effects of physical culture could offset or even outdo the benevolent effects?

directions. Smith is welcome to make himself a better man by exercising his legs three hours a day. But I prefer to sit in an armchair and exercise my soul. Smith comes in refreshed from a half-day's sojourn in the open air, and I come away refreshed from a roomful of old friends talking three at a time amidst clouds of tobacco smoke.

 7. The trouble with so many of the physical-culture devotees is that they tire out the soul in trying to serve it. I am inclined to believe that the beneficent effects of the regular quarter-hour's exercise before breakfast, is more than offset by the mental wear and tear involved in getting out of bed fifteen minutes earlier than one otherwise would. Some one has calculated that the amount of moral resolution expended in New York City every winter day in getting up to take one's cold bath would be enough to decide a dozen municipal elections in favor of the decent candidate, or to send fifty grafting legislators to jail for an average term of three and a half years. The same specialist has worked out the formula that the average married man's usefulness about the house varies inversely with his fondness for violent exercise. Smith's dumb-bell practice, for instance, leaves him no time for hanging up the pictures. After his long Sunday's walk he is invariably too tired to answer his wife's questions concerning the influence of the tariff on high prices.

 8. By this time it will be plain that I am no passionate admirer of the gospel of salvation by hygiene. So many things that the world holds precious have been developed under the most unhygienic conditions. Revolutions for the liberation of mankind have been plotted in unsanitary cellars and dungeons. Religions have taken root and prospered in catacombs[12]. Great poems have been written in stuffy garrets. Great orations have been spoken before sweating crowds in the foul air of overheated legislative chambers. Lovers are said to be fond of dark corners and out-of-the-way places. It is not by accident that children, said to be the most beautiful thing in the world, are so inordinately fond of dirt. Every great truth on its first appearance has been declared a menace to morals and society; in other words, unhygienic. And yet one would imagine that truth, from its habit of going naked, would appeal strongly to the ardent fresh-air practitioner.

16 What is the topic sentence of Paragraph 8?

17 What expressions approximately convey the meaning of dirty?

18 What figures of speech have been adopted in this paragraph to reinforce the controlling idea and deepen the thesis?

## Notes

1. preposterous /prɪˈpɒst(ə)rəs/ *a.*　contrary to reason or common sense; utterly absurd or ridiculous
2. nape /neɪp/ *n.*　the back of a person's neck
3. lunge /lʌndʒ/ *v.*　make a sudden forward thrust of the body, typically with an arm outstretched to attack someone or seize something
4. melodrama /ˈmeləˌdrɑːmə/ *n.*　a sensational dramatic piece with exaggerated characters and exciting events intended to appeal to the emotions
5. heirloom /ˈeəˌluːm/ *n.*　a valuable object that has been given by an older member of a family to a younger member of the same family, esp. one given several times in this way
6. prevarication /[prɪˈværɪˌkeɪʃən/ *n.*　an evasive way to avoid telling the truth or saying exactly what you think
7. superfluous /sjuːˈpɜːfluəs/ *a.*　more than is needed; extra and not necessary
8. diaphragm /ˈdaɪəˌfræm/ *n.*　a thin piece of material that is stretched across an opening, esp. the muscle that separates the chest from the lower part of the body containing the stomach and bowels
9. scraggy /ˈskrægi/ *a.*　very thin, especially so that the bones stick out
10. Don Quixote /dɒn kiːˈhəʊti, dɒn ˈkwɪksəʊt/　the hero of a romance (1605—1615) by Cervantes, a satirical account of chivalric beliefs and conduct. The character of Don Quixote is typified by a romantic vision and naive, unworldly idealism.
11. Falstaffian /fɔːlˈstɑːfɪən, fɒl-/ *a.*　relating to or resembling Shakespeare's character Sir John Falstaff in being fat, jolly, and debauched:
12. catacomb /ˈkætəkəʊm/ *n.*　a series of underground passages and rooms where bodies were buried in the past

## A Critical Reader (II)

1. After going through the article, what is the thesis proposed by Simeon Strunsky? Do you agree with his proposition? To what extent you approve or disapprove of his argument?
2. Try to compare/contrast your preliminary thoughts generated in the warming-up section with the argumentative points demonstrated in the article. Please structure and systemize your ideas and further bring forward more convincing counter-arguments to wrestle with author's reasoning.

# A Critical Writer

## I. Basic Writing Techniques

### 1. Style and word choice

*The Solid Flesh*, regarding the permeating physical culture among the general public, fully demonstrates the irreconcilable stance of the author Simeon Strunsky by quoting and attacking the practices of physical-culture devotees, and by presenting and advocating his own firm conviction with the ironic and sarcastic tone adopted throughout, especially in the first section where the words and deeds of the prototypical fitness enthusiasts have been either gently insinuated or even mercilessly repudiated, which is achieved by the careful choice of words. Please figure out the examples from the text to attest to the irony and sarcasm in which the confusion, discontent and even fury of the author are unveiled.

1) Why, for instance, should every system of gymnastics require that a man place himself in the most <u>ridiculous and unnatural</u> postures?

2) Equally <u>preposterous</u> is the practice of standing on one leg and stretching the other toward the nape of one's neck. In the confines of a city bedroom such evolutions are not only <u>ungraceful</u> but frequently <u>dangerous</u>.

3) Harrington's young son, who insists on being present during the <u>ordeal</u>, believes that the entire performance is intended for his <u>amusement</u>, and <u>laughs immoderately</u>.

4) Morning exercise is incompatible with the maintenance of parental dignity. Were I a child again I could neither love nor respect a father who placed two chairs at a considerable distance from each other and mounted them horizontally like the human bridge in a <u>melodrama</u>.

5) I know of one man who skipped the rope one hundred times every morning. Within four months he had lost three and a half pounds, and <u>driven</u> the family in the flat below <u>into nervous prostration</u>.

6) They will <u>exaggerate</u> the number of inches they keep their bedroom windows raised in midwinter; they will quote <u>ridiculous</u> estimates of the doctors' bills they have saved; they will represent themselves as being in the most <u>incredibly</u> perfect health.

7) I know one sober, intelligent business-man who not only habitually <u>understates</u>, by ten degrees, the temperature of his morning tub, but gives an altogether <u>distorted</u> impression of the alacrity with which he leaps into his bath every morning, and the reluctance with which he leaves it.

### 2. Basic rules for good sentences
#### 2.1 Unity

Please read the following two sentences and try to find out how unity is displayed:

Sentence 1: Smith is one of the men set apart by nature to perpetuate the Don Quixote type of beauty, just as I am doomed with the lapse of time to approximate the Falstaffian type. (Paragraph 5)

Sentence 2: Some one has calculated that the amount of moral resolution expended in New York City every winter day in getting up to take one's cold bath would be enough to decide a dozen municipal elections in favor of the decent candidate, or to send fifty grafting legislators to jail for an average term of three and a half years. (Paragraph 7)

What is the "one single, complete thought" respectively for each sentence above? And how is the "unity" actualized?

Sentence 1:

_____
_____
_____

Sentence 2:

_____
_____
_____

### 2.2 Cohesion and coherence

Please read the following sentences and try to find out how cohesion and coherence is displayed:

(1) A table is no longer something to write upon or to eat upon, but something to lie down upon while one flings out his arms and legs fifty times in four contrary directions. (Paragraph 3)

(2) I know one sober, intelligent business-man who not only habitually understates, by ten degrees, the temperature of his morning tub, but gives an altogether distorted impression of the alacrity with which he leaps into his bath every morning, and the reluctance with which he leaves it. (Paragraph 4)

(3) And not only that, but since he has gone in for exercise and fresh air and has given up smoking, his income has increased by at least 50 per cent, owing to his improved health and clearer mental vision. (Paragraph 7)

Please find out more of such examples by yourself.

### 2.3 Conciseness

Please convey the meaning of the following sentence in English:

1) 晨练是与维持父母的尊严所不相容和不协调的。如果我再次回到孩童时代，我是既不会爱戴也不会尊重一位将两把椅子摆放在距彼此相当距离的位置，然后像在一幕闹剧中的人桥一般水平地横卧于其上的父亲的。

_____
_____
_____
_____

2) 我更为相信的是早餐之前十五分钟的常规锻炼所带来的益处会被提前一刻钟起床时的精神折磨所抵消。

_____
_____
_____
_____

Now please compare what you write with the text and find out how conciseness is achieved:

Morning exercise is incompatible with the maintenance of parental dignity. Were I a child again I could neither love nor respect a father who placed two chairs at a considerable distance from each other and mounted them horizontally like the human bridge in a melodrama. (Paragraph 2)

I am inclined to believe that the beneficent effects of the regular quarter-hour's exercise before breakfast, is more than offset by the mental wear and tear involved in getting out of bed fifteen minutes earlier than one otherwise would. (Paragraph 7)

### 3. Basic rules for good paragraphs

**3.1  Please read Paragraph 6 again and do the following exercises:**

1) What's the topic sentence of Paragraph 6? How are the other sentences related to the topic sentence?

2) How are cohesion and coherence displayed and achieved?

**3.2  Analysis:**

1) Unity:

Paragraph 6 well exemplifies the unity of a paragraph with the Sentence 5 functioning as the topic sentence and thereby the core of the paragraph, and with other sentences clustering around to transit to or elaborate on the controlling idea "approaching the same goal from two different directions." Throughout the paragraph, these "two different directions" are either pointed out explicitly as the underlined from Sentence 1 to Sentence 5 to present the theoretical and logical argumentation, or illustrated by the vivid and tangible daily anecdotes quoted from Sentence 6 through Sentence 8 to buttress the argument.

Sentence 1: I do not, of course, mean to deny <u>the ancient tradition</u> that a sound body makes a sound mind.

Sentence 2: But I would only point out that we are just beginning to wake to the truth of <u>the converse proposition</u>, that a sane, equable, easy-going mind keeps the body well.

Sentence 3: Hence there are really <u>two kinds of exercise, and two kinds of hygiene</u>, a physical kind and a spiritual kind.

Sentence 4: <u>Which one</u> a man will choose should be left entirely to himself.

Sentence 5: It is only a question of approaching the same goal from <u>two different directions</u>.

Sentence 6: Smith is welcome to make himself a better man by exercising his legs three hours a day.

Sentence 7: But I prefer to sit in an armchair and exercise my soul.

Sentence 8: Smith comes in refreshed from a half-day's sojourn in the open air, and I come away refreshed from a roomful of old friends talking three at a time amidst clouds of tobacco smoke.

2) Cohesion:

The relationship among the sentences is lucid and clear and therefore the development of the paragraph is trackable. Such aforementioned expressions underscored as "the ancient tradition", "the converse proposition", "two kinds of exercise", "two kinds of hygiene", "which one", and "two different directions" don't only effect the unity with regards to the preset topic, but also attain the cohesion throughout the paragraph by respectively pointing to one side or juxtaposing the two sides, since the semantic coherence and syntactic cohesion is the cornerstone of the unity. And besides, it is further reinforced by some common but precise connective words to guide readers through the transition and progress of the argumentation, for instance, "but" in Sentence 2 to bring forward the opposite thought, "hence" to bring the controversy to a reconciliation to be supported by the following reasoning.

3) Coherence:

Sentence 1 is transition from the preceding paragraphs that "the ancient tradition" is sensible and therefore indisputable, but it is the only one sided and biased statement if without the equal attention attached to the "the converse proposition" in Sentence 2. The prior unbalanced focus has almost dismissed the latter proposal and even set up the opposition between these two propositions, which is absolutely misleading and fallacious from the point of view of the author, conversely these two alternatives are paralleled and compatible with each other without either of them outmatching the other. So in Sentence 3, 4 and 5 the author firmly maintains that mankind, faced with "two kinds of exercise, two kinds of hygiene" in the pursuit of health and well-being, is endowed with the inalienable freedom to make a choice between "two different directions" at will. What follows from Sentence 6 to 8 is the contrasted experiences of Smith and the author yet with equally desirable outcomes to validate the "approaching the same goal from two different directions" —All roads lead to Rome.

### 3.3 Imitation

1) 我当然并不否认西药对于治愈特定疾病方面的巨大功效，而只是想指出我们也应当认同中药在养生、调理和除病方面的作用。所以，存在两种方案，一种是以微观的方式消除疾病的症状和引发的具体原因，另一种则从宏观上调节和重新恢复机体的平衡、从而逐步消除局部的病灶。在病痛缠绕之时，究竟选择哪种药物和治疗方式取决于病情的发展和本人的偏好。这只是通往健康的两种和而不同的方式。

2) 我并不否认美丽的面容和姣好的身材有助于一个女生在激烈的就业竞争中占得先机,而只是想指出,拥有一个充满学识和智慧的头脑也能助女生拔得头筹。因而,通向职场的道路上有两种选择,两种准备,一种是通过医学整容技术来改善自己外在的容颜,另一种是通过充实内在的储存来面对挑战。你准备选择哪种方式呢?

_____
_____
_____
_____
_____

### 4. Basic rule for good essays

#### 4.1 Questions

1) What is the structure of this essay?
2) What is the thesis proposed by the author?
3) In what way does the author argue for the thesis?

#### 4.2 Analysis

This essay is well-organized with a clear structure that allows the author's exposition and argumentation to flow with ease.

**Part One (Paragraph 1—5):** <u>Lead-in by examples</u> which are the various anecdotes quoted from the acquaintances, friends of the author and the author himself to be set up as the target attacked one by one.

**Paragraph 1** designates the physical culture as the topic, sets the ironic and sarcastic tone toward the topic and demonstrates the general attitude toward it—a kind of disgust and repugnance.

**Paragraph 2** introduces the anecdote of Harrington to demonstrate that "morning exercise is incompatible with the maintenance of parental dignity".

**Paragraph 3** illustrates with the cases of one man and the author himself that the confusion home exercise introduces into the world of common things when the ordinary household furniture are utilized as the fitness apparatus.

**Paragraph 4** refers to the story of "one sober, intelligent business-man" to indicate that "people will lose all sense of truthfulness when they speak of physical culture and fresh air".

**Paragraph 5** vindicates with example of Smith that the physical exertion is helpless to the loss of weight and the slenderness of figure that is preordained and built in genes.

**Part Two (Paragraph 6—7):** <u>Development by direct reasoning</u> to refute the physical culture on the whole

**Paragraph 6** In addition to the widely-admitted ancient tradition, the converse proposition makes sense that a sound mind makes a sound body, both of which are accessible to people. (The counter-proposal as the alternative is pointed out to dismiss the original statement as the only way.)

**Paragraph 7** The positive effects of physical culture are offset and even defeated by the inescapable downsides. (Further attacks inflicted on the old belief to question and even demolish the validity of the original statement.)

**Part Three (Paragraph 8)** The conclusion with the ultimate thesis statement brought out—"Many things that the world holds precious have been developed under the most unhygienic conditions."

### 4.3 Working out an outline:

Please work out an outline on the topic "Traditional Chinese Medicine and Western Medicine" according to the analysis above. You may resort to the "Writing Process" in the Introduction of this book. Your writing plan should address at least the following questions:

1) How many parts and paragraphs do you plan to write?

2) What is the main idea for each paragraph?

3) What kind of examples will you use to illustrate the typical features of these two types of medication?

## II. Specific Writing Techniques

### 1. Inductive and deductive writing strategy

With the writing topic designated and fixed down, you are always faced with two alternatives of writing forms—inductive organization or deductive organization. The inductive writing pattern moves from the specific to the general with the statistics, observations, particular encounters and experiences as the specific examples and evidences leading to the general statement and final conclusion that comes at the end of an essay; conversely, the deductive writing strategy proceeds from the general to the specific with the thesis statement forthright delivered at the beginning, and then illustrated and enumerated by the following arguments in the remainder of the essay.

*The Solid Flesh* obviously adopts the inductive writing mode with the thesis statement brought forward in the last paragraph "Many things that the world holds precious have been developed under the most unhygienic conditions." From Paragraph 1 through Paragraph 5 a series of anecdotal stories are introduced to respectively reveal 4 negatives and shortcomings of physical culture, and then by way of Paragraph 6 and Paragraph 7 that further expose the downsides, the conclusion Paragraph 8 pushes all the arguments into the ultimate climax with the thesis generated. The inductive writing mode adopted by the author here well fits into the proposed thesis that is controversial and contradictory to the public opinion, and therefore as likely as not to be refuted and resisted by the potential reader who could have put the essay aside at the sight of the such distasteful and offending conclusion. In order to reduce such resistance, the revolutionary conclusion is well preceded by some ubiquitous daily examples and by author's rebuttal one by one that dismantles readers' mental vigilance and pave the way for the coming of the concluding statement.

However, the adoption of such a winding route to the thesis is compatibly blended with the unreserved irony conveyed in a variety of linguistic expressions and with the straightforwardness and directness demonstrated in some paragraphs, such as, Paragraph 4, 6, 7, 8, which adopt the opposing pattern—the deductive writing organization.

**2. Figure of speech**

In the concluding paragraph, what kind of rhetoric devices could you figure out by means of which author gives the prominence to the theme?

**Paragraph 8:**

By this time it will be plain that I am no passionate admirer of the gospel of salvation by hygiene. So many things that the world holds precious have been developed under the most unhygienic conditions. Revolutions for the liberation of mankind have been plotted in unsanitary cellars and dungeons. Religions have taken root and prospered in catacombs. Great poems have been written in stuffy garrets. Great orations have been spoken before sweating crowds in the foul air of overheated legislative chambers. Lovers are said to be fond of dark corners and out-of-the-way places. It is not by accident that children, said to be the most beautiful thing in the world, are so inordinately fond of dirt. Every great truth on its first appearance has been declared a menace to morals and society; in other words, unhygienic. And yet one would imagine that truth, from its habit of going naked, would appeal strongly to the ardent fresh-air practitioner.

1) **Paradox**—the seemingly self-contradicting statement that actually makes sense with underlying meaning after careful deliberation.

*So many things that the world holds precious have been developed under the most unhygienic conditions.*

2) **Parallelism**—words, phrases, clauses, or sentences are arranged in a number of similar structures so as to give the whole a definite pattern and intensify the emotions and highlight the thesis.

*Revolutions for the liberation of mankind have been plotted in unsanitary cellars and dungeons. // Religions have taken root and prospered in catacombs. // Great poems have* been written in stuffy garrets. // Great orations have been spoken before sweating crowds in the foul air of overheated legislative chambers. // Lovers are said to be fond of dark corners and out-of-the-way places. // It is not by accident that children, said to be the most beautiful thing in the world, are so inordinately fond of dirt. // Every great truth on its first appearance has been declared a menace to morals and society; in other words, unhygienic. And yet one would imagine that truth, from its habit of going naked, would appeal strongly to the ardent fresh-air practitioner.

Can you come up with a paradoxical conclusion, that is, the seemingly contradicting statement on the surface but with the harmonious essence and the indisputable truth at the core, which then could be supported and illustrated with a series of examples presented in a parallel structure?

**Tips:**

Here are some epigrams with the paradox embedded; you can choose one of them as the topic sentence in your paragraph to be followed by your selected examples.

*More haste, less speed.*

*The farthest way about is the nearest way home.*

*The greatest hate springs from the greatest love.*

*Cheapest is the dearest.*

*One has to be cruel to be kind.*

## III. Your Turn to Write

Please write an essay with the thesis that Chinese Traditional Medicine is more favorable to the recovery of physical health than its western counterpart. The inductive structure should be adopted with Part One focused on the preference for western medicine by modern people through a series of instances and examples, then Part Two devoted to your arguments and rebuttal against the phenomenon and finally Part Three presenting your final thematic statement to effectively conclude your argumentation. Remember that in the first part of illustration your stance is not neutral but firmly opposite to the overuse and even abuse of the western doses of medication by launching your small-scale counter-attack one by one, which could prepares you for the comprehensive arguments in the second part and eventually leads to your final statement.

### Pearls of Wisdom

1. Happiness lies, first of all, in health. —George William Curtis

2. A healthy mind is in a healthy body. —Juvenal

3. Cheerfulness is health; its opposite, melancholy, is disease. —Thomas Chandler Haliburton

4. A light heart lives long. —William Shakespeare

5. Diseases of the soul are more dangerous than those of the body. —Marcus Tullius Cicero

## Text B

**Warming up**

1. When do you usually go to bed?
2. When your bedtime approaches, what is your regular reaction, happily or reluctantly consigning yourself to the encroaching drowsiness, or unwaveringly wrestling with the sleepiness to lengthen the time of day?
3. Sleeping is a routine practice to repeat every day, an assignment to finish, an enjoyment to expect, a luxury hardly to afford for you, or something else in your eyes?

### On Going to Bed

by Christopher Morley

**A Critical Reader (I)**

1. One of the characters in *The Moon and Sixpence* remarked that he had faithfully lived up to the old precept about doing every day two things you heartily *dislike*; for, said he, every day he had got up and he had gone to bed.

2. It is a sad thing that as soon as the hands of the clock have turned ten the shadow of going to bed begins to creep over the evening. We have *never* heard bedtime spoken of *with any enthusiasm*. One after another we have seen a gathering disperse, each person saying (with *an air of solemn resignation*): "Well, I guess I'll go to bed." But there was *no hilarity*[1] about it. It is really rather touching how they *cling to* the departing skirts of the day that is vanishing under the spinning shadow of night.

[1] What is the attitude of the author towards the impending bedtime? What kind of expressions could denote that standpoint?

3. This is odd, we repeat, for sleep is highly popular among human beings. The reluctance to go to one's couch is not at all a reluctance to slumber, for almost all of us will doze happily in an armchair or on a sofa, or even festooned[2] on the floor with a couple of cushions. But the actual and formal yielding to sheets and blankets is to be postponed to the last possible moment.

4. The devil of drowsiness is at his most potent, we find, about 10:30 P.M. At this period the human carcass[3] seems to consider that it has finished its cycle, which began with so much courage nearly sixteen hours before. *It begins to slack and the mind halts on a dead centre every now and then, refusing to complete the revolution.* Now there are those who hold that this is certainly the seemly and appointed time to go to bed and they do so as a matter of routine. These are, commonly, the happier creatures, for they take the tide of sleep at the flood and are borne calmly and with gracious gentleness out to great waters of nothingness. They push off from the wharf on a tranquil current and nothing more is to be seen or heard of these voyagers until they reappear at the breakfast table, digging lustily into their grapefruit.

5. These people are happy, aye, in a brutish and sedentary[4] fashion, but they miss the admirable adventures of those more embittered wrestlers who will not give in without a struggle. These latter suffer severe pangs between 10:30 and about 11:15 while they grapple[5] with their fading faculties and seek to reestablish the will on its tottering throne. This requires courage stout, valor unbending. Once you yield, be it ever so little, to the tempter, you are lost. And here our poor barren clay plays us false, undermining the intellect with many a trick and wile[6]. "I will sit down for a season in that comfortable chair," the creature says to himself, "and read this sprightly novel. That will ease my mind and put me in humour for a continuance of lively thinking." And the end of that man is a steady nasal buzz from the bottom of the chair where he has collapsed, an unsightly object and a disgrace to humanity. This also means a big bill from the electric light company at the end of the month. In many such ways will his corpse betray him, leading him by plausible self-deceptions into a pitfall of sleep, whence he is aroused about 3

2. Why does there exist such a difference between "the casual and informal surrendering to an armchair and sofa" and "actual and formal yielding to sheets and blanket" on your mind?

3. What physiological signals and portents would foreshadow the impending bedtime?

4. Who are the "happier creatures" and "embittered wrestlers"? From the author's perspective, who are more fortunate and admirable, the former or the latter one?

5. What is the "trick and wile" our poor barren clay plays on us?

6. What are the suggested methods to distance from and defeat drowsiness?

A.M. when the planet turns over on the other side. Only by stiff perseverance and rigid avoidance of easy chairs may the critical hour between 10:30 and 11:30 be safely passed. Tobacco, a self-brewed pot of tea, and a browsing along bookshelves (remain standing and do not sit down with your book) are helps in this time of struggle. Even so, there are some happily drowsy souls who can never cross these shallows alone without grounding on the Lotus Reefs. Our friend J-D-K-, magnificent creature, was (when we lived with him) so potently hypnophil[7] that, even erect and determined as his bookcase and urgently bent upon Brann's *Iconoclast*[8] or some other literary irritant, sleep would seep through his pores and he would fall with a crash, lying there in unconscious bliss until someone came in and prodded him up, reeling and ashamed.

6. But, as we started to say, those who survive this drastic weeding out which Night imposes upon her wooers—so as to cull and choose only the truly meritorious[9] lovers—experience supreme delights which are unknown to their snoring fellows. When the struggle with somnolence[10] has been fought out and won, when the world is all-covering darkness and close-pressing silence, when the tobacco suddenly takes on fresh vigour and fragrance and the books lie strewn about the table, then *it seems as though all the rubbish and floating matter of the day's thoughts have poured away and only the bright, clear, and swift current of the mind itself remains, flowing happily and without impediment.* This perfection of existence is not to be reached very often; but when properly approached it may be won. It is a different mind that one uncovers then, *a spirit which is lucid and hopeful*, to which (for a few serene hours) time exists not. *The friable*[11] *resolutions of the day are brought out again and recemented and chiselled*[12] *anew. Surprising schemes are started and carried through to happy conclusion, lifetimes of amazement are lived in a few passing ticks.* There is one who at such moments resolves, with complete sincerity, to start at one end of the top shelf and read again all the books in his library, intending this time really to extract their true marrow[13]. He takes a clean sheet of paper and sets down memoranda of all the people he intends to write to, and all the plumbers and what not that he will call up the next day. And the next time this happy seizure attacks him he will go through the same gestures again without surprise

[7] After the battle with the somnolence is won, what kind of wonderland is discovered based on the author's description?

and without the slightest mortification[14]. And then, having lived a generation of good works since midnight struck, he summons all his resolution and goes to bed.

## Notes

1. hilarity /hi'lærəti/ *n.* extreme amusement, especially when expressed by laughter: his incredulous expression was the cause of much hilarity
2. festoon /fes'tu:n/ *v.* to decorate a place or thing with strips of cloth or chains of paper, lights, flowers, etc.
3. carcass /'kɑ:kəs/ *n.* the body of a dead animal
4. sedentary /'sednˌteri/ *a.* (of a person) tending to spend much time seated; somewhat inactive
5. grapple /'græpəl/ *v.* to engage in a close fight or struggle without weapons; wrestle
6. wile /wail/ *a.* devious or cunning stratagems employed in manipulating or persuading someone to do what one wants
7. hypnophil /hip'nəʊfil/ *n.* the obsession with sleeping; the antonym of hypnophobia.
8. iconoclast /ai'kɔnəklast/ *n.* a person who strongly opposes generally accepted beliefs and traditions
9. meritorious /mɛri'tɔ:riəs/ *a.* deserving reward or praise
10. somnolence /'sɔmnələns/ *n.* sleepiness, drowsiness
11. friable /'fraiəbəl/ *a.* easily crumbled or pulverized
12. chisel /'tʃiz(ə)l/ *v.* to cut or shape (something) with a chisel, a long-bladed hand tool with a bevelled cutting edge and a handle which is struck with a hammer or mallet, used to cut or shape wood, stone, or metal
13. marrow /'mærəʊ/ *n.* the innermost, essential, or choicest part; pith
14. mortification /ˌmɔ:təfi'keiʃən/ *n.* great embarrassment and shame

## A Critical Reader (II)

1. When is the bedtime for the author inferred from the article?
2. Are you "embittered wrestlers" or "the happier creatures" under the attack of the aggressive drowsiness? Have you undergone the tortuous struggle and defeated the haunting sleepiness and sluggishness? If yes, are you in the same physical and psychological condition as the one pictured by author? If no, do you subscribe to the author's belief that wonderland is discovered not by consigning yourself to the natural summon—going to

bed instinctively ushered by the sleepiness, but by the unrelenting fight against the natural call to readjust the biological clock built in our body? So what is your wonderland in the disturbed quietude and pervasive darkness?

3. From the argumentation of author, it is observed that the struggle and battle between the nature and human will is the permanent theme that is not only reflected on such a macro scale as the complicated relationship between the human society and the natural environment around us, but also demonstrated in such micro daily routine as the appropriate bedtime which should be determined by the physiology (nature) or by our volition. So from such a perspective that implicates the relationship between mankind and nature, what is your new reflection on our daily life practices?

## A Critical Writer

### I. Style and Word Choice

1. This essay is simply but lucidly titled as *On Going to Bed*, the different expressions synonymous with "going to bed" are adopted to attain the diversity and achieve the cohesion and unity on the level of diction, though. Can you find, in this essay, as many various expressions as possible, both direct and indirect, both literary and figurative?

This is odd, we repeat, for <u>sleep</u> is highly popular among human beings.

The reluctance to <u>go to one's couch</u> is not at all a reluctance to <u>slumber</u>, for almost all of us will <u>doze</u> happily in an armchair or on a sofa, or even festooned on the floor with a couple of cushions.

But <u>the actual and formal yielding to sheets and blankets</u> is to be postponed to the last possible moment.

These are, commonly, the happier creatures, for they take the tide of sleep at the flood and are <u>borne</u> calmly and with gracious gentleness out <u>to great waters of nothingness</u>. They <u>push off from the wharf on a tranquil current</u> and nothing more is to be seen or heard of these voyagers until they reappear at the breakfast table, digging lustily into their grapefruit.

The end of that man is <u>a steady nasal buzz from the bottom of the chair</u> where he has collapsed, an unsightly object and a disgrace to humanity.

Sleep would seep through his pores and he would fall with a crash, <u>lying there in unconscious bliss</u> until someone came in and prodded him up, reeling and ashamed.

2. The essay probes into a commonplace phenomenon—going to bed, which at the first sight of the title, could evoke readers' association with the physiological exposition; on the contrary, it is far from the monotonous scientific explanation but characterized with the vivid and lively tone by means of the literary implement, here typically referring to the application of the metaphor and personification, to comment on this familiar topic with a special but interesting perspective and to

convince the readers of the incomparable delights after the lingering drowsiness shattered.

**Metaphor**—A figure of speech in which an implied comparison is made between two unlike things that actually have something in common.

**Personification**—A figure of speech in which an inanimate object or abstraction is given human qualities or abilities.

Try to figure out some examples of these rhetoric devices.

*These are, commonly, the happier creatures, for they take the tide of sleep at the flood and are borne calmly and with gracious gentleness out to great waters of nothingness. They push off from the wharf on a tranquil current and nothing more is to be seen or heard of these voyagers until they reappear at the breakfast table, digging lustily into their grapefruit.* (Metaphor)

*These people are happy, aye, in a brutish and sedentary fashion, but they miss the admirable adventures of those more embittered wrestlers who will not give in without a struggle. These latter suffer severe pangs between 10:30 and about 11:15 while they grapple with their fading faculties and seek to reestablish the will on its tottering throne.* (Metaphor)

*As we started to say, those who survive this drastic weeding out which Night imposes upon her wooers—so as to cull and choose only the truly meritorious lovers—experience supreme delights which are unknown to their snoring fellows.* (Personification)

## II. Good Structure in the Level of Paragraph and Essay

### 1. Questions
1) How many parts does the essay consist of? What are they?
2) What is their respective function in the development of the argumentation?
3) How is the semantic coherence achieved throughout?

### 2. Analysis
**2.1  The essay is structured in two parts.**

**Part One (Paragraph 1—3)** is the focused introduction to reveal the general topic (_sleep/ going to bed) by quotation and further limit and clarify it in the words of "actual and formal yielding to the sheets and blankets" so as to pave the way for the more focused argumentation afterwards.

**Part Two (Paragraph 4—6)** is an effective development with the thematic conclusion embedded in the course of argumentation. In face of drowsiness, the "happier creatures" obediently and docilely subjected to the natural drowsiness without struggle and therefore submerged into the boundless darkness and serenity of night; and further transfers to the "embittered wrestlers" who fight through the formidable sleepiness imposed by the night and eventually discover the new land of amazement, hope and happiness unknown to the former submissive and meek subjects of night.

**2.2** Throughout the essay, the first sentence of each paragraph plays a crucial role of either transit point where the old information is shifted to the new and the known to the unknown, or the topic sentence which illuminates what follows, or both. Could you analyze the first sentences from Paragraph 2 through 6 to get a closer look at how the cohesion and coherence is achieved throughout?

**Paragraph 2:** It is <u>a sad thing</u> that as soon as the hands of the clock have turned ten <u>the shadow of going to bed</u> begins to creep over the evening. ("going to bed" repeats the old information and "a sad thing" further reveals the author's attitude and therefore is new and unknown.)

**Paragraph 3:** <u>This</u> is <u>odd</u>, we repeat, for sleep is <u>highly popular</u> among human beings. ("This" refer to the sad feeling—"solemn resignation" by adopting reference, exactly speaking, the pronoun; and "odd" further poses the question and doubt of such a sentiment.)

**Paragraph 4:** (a paragraph of importance, as a transit point, where the phenomenon "going to bed" is further transferred to what drags people to the bed)

<u>The devil of drowsiness</u> is at his most potent, we find, about <u>10:30 P.M.</u>

**Paragraph 5:** <u>These people are happy</u>, aye, in a brutish and sedentary fashion, but they <u>miss the admirable adventures of those more embittered wrestlers</u> who will not give in without a struggle. (The opening sentence denotes a shift from "these people" with reference to "the happier creatures who take the tide of sleep in the Paragraph 4" to the new focus on how "admirable adventurer" battle with the sleepiness)

**Paragraph 6:** But, as we started to say, <u>those who survive this drastic weeding out</u> which Night imposes upon her wooers—so as to cull and choose only the truly meritorious lovers—<u>experience supreme delights</u> which are unknown to their snoring fellows. ("who survive this drastic weeding out" is the substitute for "admirable adventurer" mentioned in the preceding paragraph, and here further revealed are the delights awaiting these adventures.)

## III. Your Turn to Write

Going to bed is a normal routine we will do and repeat every day but not without some struggle between our physiological somnolence and mental willpower, so how about getting up? Do you always undergo a fierce battle at this moment to make a choice, surrendering yourself to the overwhelming sleepiness therefore to elongate the nighttime and your beautiful dream, or defeating the excessive drowsiness with will and resolution therefore to jump out of the bed and start a new day earlier? Please write a composition titled "On Getting Up", in which you are supposed to imitate author's reasoning pattern to briefly present the advantage of one side (to get up earlier or later), and transfer to the merits of the other side which you stand up for as your preference.

## Pearls of Wisdom

1. Early to bed and early to rise, makes a man healthy, wealthy and wise.
—Benjamin Franklin

2. If you're going to do something tonight that you'll be sorry for tomorrow morning...sleep late. —Henny Youngman

3. The bed is a bundle of paradoxes: we go to it with reluctance, yet we quit it with regret; we make up our minds every night to leave it early, but we make up our bodies every morning to keep it late. —Charles Caleb Colton

4. Sleep is the interest we have to pay on the capital which is called in at death; and the higher the rate of interest and the more regularly it is paid, the further the date of redemption is postponed. —Arthur Schopenhauer

# Text C

## Agony From Ecstasy

by Lynn Smith

**A Critical Reader**

1. I hear a lot of people talking about Ecstasy[1], calling it a fun, harmless drug. All I can think is, "if they only knew."

2. I grew up in a small, rural town in Pennsylvania. It's one of those places where everyone knows your name, what you did, what you ate and so on. I was a straight-A student and one of the popular kids, liked by all the different crowds. Drugs never played a part in my life. They were never a question—I was too involved and focused on other things.

3. I always dreamed of moving to New York City to study acting and pursue a career in theater. My dream came true when my mom brought me to the city to attend acting school. As you can imagine, it was quite a change from home.

4. I was exposed to new people, new ideas and a completely new way of life—a way of life that exposed me to drugs. Most of the people that I met in the acting school had already been doing drugs for years. I felt that by using drugs, I would become a part of their world and it would deepen my friendships with them to new levels. I tried pot[2], even a little cocaine[3], but it was Ecstasy that changed my life forever.

**1** What does the author mean by saying, "if they only knew"?

**2** What are the circumstances of your growth, the countryside, suburb or downtown? A place with high mobility of inhabitants or great stability of residents? A community of acquaintances or of strangers? And what does it impact on your living styles, personality or even outlook?

**3** What change does moving to New York bring to her?

5. I remember the feeling I had the first time I did Ecstasy: complete and utter bliss. I could feel the pulse of the universe. It was as if I had unlocked some sort of secret world; it was as if I'd found heaven. And I wondered how anything that made you feel so good could possibly be bad.

6. As time went by, things changed. I graduated, and began to use drugs, especially Ecstasy, more frequently. As I did, I actually started to look down on those who did not. I surrounded myself only with those who did. I had gone from a girl who never used drugs to a woman who couldn't imagine life without them.

7. In five months, I went from a person living somewhat responsibly while pursuing my dream to a person who didn't care about a thing—and the higher I got, the deeper I sank into a dark, lonely place. When I did sleep, I had nightmares and the shakes. I had pasty skin, a throbbing[4] head and the beginnings of paranoia[5], but I ignored it all, thinking it was normal until the night I thought I was dying.

8. On this night, I was sitting on the couch with my friends, watching a movie and feeling normal when suddenly, I felt as if I needed to jump out of my skin. Racing thoughts, horrible images and illusions crept through my mind. I thought I was seeing the devil, and I repeatedly asked my friends if I was dead. On top of all this, I felt as if I was having a heart attack. Somehow, I managed to pick up the telephone and call my mom in the middle of the night, telling her to come get me. She did, pulling me out of my apartment the next morning.

9. I didn't know who I was or where I was as my mom drove me back to my family's hospital in Pennsylvania. I spent most of the drive curled up in the back seat while my younger sister tried to keep me calm.

10. I spent the next 14 days in the hospital in a state of extreme confusion. This is what Ecstasy gave me—but it didn't stop there. My doctors performed a scan of my brain. I couldn't believe my eyes when I saw the results. The scan showed several dark marks on the image of my brain, and my doctors told me those were areas—areas that carry out memory functions—where the activity of my brain had been changed in some way.

11. Since I saw that scan, my life has been an uphill crawl.

---

[4] In what way is she involved in the circle of new friends? And what is your usual approach to engage yourself in a new friendship?

[5] Which sentence functions as the turning point from the thrilling sentiments to the discomforting bodily and mental reactions?

[6] What did Ecstasy eventually do to her?

[7] What does the author mean by "my life has been an uphill crawl"?

[8] Why does the author say that she is "one of the lucky ones"?

12. I hear people say Ecstasy is a harmless, happy drug. There's nothing happy about the way that "harmless" drug chipped away at[6] my life. Ecstasy took my strength, my motivation, my dreams, my friends, my apartment, my money and most of all, my sanity. I worry about my future and my health every day. I have many mountains ahead of me, but I plan to keep climbing because I'm one of the lucky ones.

13. I've been given a second chance, and that's not something that everyone gets.

### Notes

1. ecstasy /ˈekstəsi/ *n.*   a powerful drug that acts as a stimulant and can produce hallucinations
2. pot /pɔt/ *n.*   (slang) marijuana; the most commonly used illicit drug; considered a soft drug, it consists of the dried leaves of the hemp plant; smoked or chewed for euphoric effect
3. cocaine /kə(u)ˈkein/ *n.*   a narcotic extracted from coca leaves; used as a surface anesthetic or taken for pleasure; can become powerfully addictive
4. throbbing /ˈθrɔbiŋ/   pounding or beating strongly or violently
5. paranoia /ˌpærəˈnɔiə/ *n.*   (psychiatry) a form of schizophrenia characterized by a slowly progressive deterioration of the personality, involving delusions and often hallucinations
6. chip away at: to reduce or make progress on something incrementally

## A Critical Writer

### I. Question for Discussion:

1. Since a drug the topic the essay focuses on, it is addressed and mentioned in an array of diverse expressions throughout in order to avoid the humdrum and monotony occasioned by the repetition. Please forage the essay for a collection of drug-related words and phrases.

2. The essay is a truthful documentation of author's personal intimate experience with the drug—the gradual degradation and ultimate self-awakening. The whole addictive depravation is recorded by the descriptive details of the physical symptoms and mental reactions so as to invite the readers to witness or even undergo the temporary ups and eventual downs of her tangle with drugs. Please find out chronologically the physical and mental symptoms after her addiction to drug.

| Physical | Mental |
|---|---|
|  |  |
|  |  |
|  |  |
|  |  |
|  |  |
|  |  |
|  |  |
|  |  |

**3.** The author narrates her personal story in the first-person voice "I", that she was gradually devoured by drugs so as to lose her health and sanity, with the aim to reveal the theme of agony from Ecstasy—the fleeting and momentary rapture at the expense of the perpetually haunting anguish and misery inflicted on your body and mind. The narration is developed in the normal chronological sequence, that is, the event is presented and unfolded in accordance with the time in which it occurred. Can you figure out the transitional signs of time throughout the whole essay to better understand its layout and organization?

## II. Your Turn to Write

With reference to the autobiographic reflection of author's addition to the drug, you are expected to write your addition to such external temptations in the modern world as alcohol, smoking, computer games, digital / electronic products, your obsession with some acquired habits and interests, or your devotion to such special people as the admirable celebrity or the beloved sweetheart. The first-voice and chronological narration should be employed to genuinely reflect your fascination with the stuff where your heart was (is / has been being) captured therefore some physical and mental responses and symptoms are aroused.

## Pearls of Wisdom

1. The real question is why are millions of people so unhappy, so bored, so unfulfilled, that they are willing to drink, snort, inject or inhale any substance that might blot out reality and give them a bit of temporary relief.

—Ann1Landers

2. Anyway, no drug, not even alcohol, causes the fundamental ills of society. If we're looking for the source of our troubles, we shouldn't test people

for drugs, we should test them for stupidity, ignorance, greed and love of power.

—Patrick Jake O'Rourke

3. Drug misuse is not a disease; it is a decision, like the decision to step out in front of a moving car. You would call that not a disease but an error of judgment. —Philip K. Dick

4. A strong positive attitude will create more miracles than any wonder drug. —Patricia Neal

5. There is only one reason why men become addicted to drugs, they are weak men. Only strong men are cured, and they cure themselves.

—Martin H. Fischer

# Corpus-based Exercises (6)

## I. Key Word: sleep

1. *Sleep* is the theme of Text B, although it is referred to in the diverse expressions which effectively avoid the tedious repetition for one thing, and achieve the coherence and unity throughout for another. However, considering that sleep is a common, frequently used and therefore important word, it is not unnecessary to have a good command of its various collocations in order to add color and vigor to "sleep". What is your store of expressions and idioms related to *sleep*? Please list out from your memory as many as possible?

2. Below are the concordance lines of *sleep* taken from a corpus of English texts, from which some recommendable fixed expressions are summarized for your reference in the following translation exercise.

| | | | |
|---|---|---|---|
| ould include regular meals, adequate | sleep | and time with one's family . Exercise , | |
| morning Henry awoke from a deep | sleep | beneath a warm comforter , his eyes fill | |
| orning before we both fell into a deep | sleep | , her paw resting gently on my shoulder | |
| are ecstatic ./That night , I didn't | sleep | a wink . I checked my gear over and ov | |
| tsteps , I jumped into bed and feigned | sleep | . And as soon as the guard passed , I go | 5 |
| It's well known that obesity impairs | sleep | , so perhaps people get fat first and slee | |
| r . " We've found that if you 're in | sleep | deficit , performance suffers , " says Dr | |
| as a non-prescription pill for inducing | sleep | . " E Z SLEEP " had been expensive to | |
| and that I'm in them . I retreat into | sleep | ; Isleep through the day and the night , | |
| , patients weren't driven into a long | sleep | and could breathe on their own sooner . | 10 |

| | | |
|---|---|---|
| ne look at these images without losing | **sleep** | ?/And eyes , my God , eyes . Eyes |
| ost doctors agree that a healthy dose of | **sleep** | is at least seven hours , preferably |
| of catching up to reverse the effects of | **sleep** | loss , " says Dr Charles P . Pollak , head |
| over the Sudanese desert , snatches of | **sleep** | came . He supposed it was sleep . p |
| it refreshes and frequently procures | **sleep** | . A very large bed that will admit a rem |
| , I'd have trouble getting back to | **sleep** | . I'd review all the facts of the case and |
| y parents' objections , I go back to | **sleep** | , and I miss some of the most magnifice |
| to calm her until eventually she fell to | **sleep** | in my arms ./' You will have to coo |
| d she had some difficulty in getting to | **sleep** | , so she habitually spent the hours from |
| retch out more comfortably and go to | **sleep** | ./The only way he could think of w |
| lk songs . Sometimes I'd sing her to | **sleep** | . Other times I'd read her stories . I'd b |
| read-The Wealth of Nations-puts him to | **sleep** | ./Kevin dreams it is 1835 , an |
| ky I was . After I had cried myself to | **sleep** | , she had written me a note . The day nu |
| a business , or it can bore them to | **sleep** | , driving them to your competitors whi |

| | | |
|---|---|---|
| awake from a sleep | impair sleep | adequate sleep |
| bore sb. to sleep | induce sleep | a healthy dose of sleep |
| cry oneself to sleep | lose sleep | |
| drive into a long sleep | procure sleep | snatches of sleep |
| drive into a long sleep | retreat into sleep | |
| fall into a deep sleep | retreat into sleep | sleep deficit |
| feign sleep | sing sb. to sleep | sleep loss |
| get (back) to sleep | sleep a wink | |
| go (back) to sleep | | |

**3. Please translate the following Chinese sentences into English using collocations and expressions of *sleep* you have learned from the above concordance lines.**

1) 晚间睡眠缺乏会导致白天精神颓废、反应迟钝和注意力分散。

2) 这种照本宣科的教学方法不仅使学生失去主动参与的积极性，而且让学生有一种自然的抵触感，使得很多学生在这样的课堂犯困。

3) 在小睡片刻之后，他总算从饮酒的迷醉状态中清醒过来。

4) 一个热水澡、一杯温牛奶和一首舒缓的歌曲是有助于睡眠的。

5) 深夜里楼下那对新婚夫妇喧闹的吵架声惊扰了很多人的美梦。

6) 为了避开我的室友，我一整天都在外面闲逛；到了晚上，我也很早就上床，装出一副睡着的样子。

---

**4. Health tips regarding *sleep* quoted from the corpus.**

1) Just one bad night's sleep can make a person less efficient in mental tasks. Worse still, the effects of sleep loss are cumulative. A person who chronically sleeps 90 minutes less per night than is necessary will feel far worse on Friday than on Tuesday. "By the fifth night, you've lost 7.5 hours, or virtually a whole night's sleep," says psychologist Dinges. "That's the day when you're just praying to get through it."

2) Perrone also suggests exercising as a way to make your sleep schedule more regular. Working out each day will make your body crave regular rest, whereas a totally inactive day—a day spent sitting on the couch watching TV and chatting it up or sitting in front of a computer surfing the web—can cause you to have more irregular sleeping tendencies. Physical activity brings about normal body responses to sleep. Exercise will help do the trick.

3) If, after exercise, we feed sparingly, the digestion will be easy and good, the body lightsome, the temper cheerful, and all the animal functions performed agreeably. Sleep, when it follows, will be natural and undisturbed, while indolence, with full feeding, occasions nightmares and horrors inexpressible; we fall from precipices, are assaulted by wild beasts, murderers, and demons, and experience every variety of distress.

4) Our unconscious desires perhaps not even fully known to us are processed, repackaged in symbolism and presented in dreams. The inner voice sometimes demands to be heard. Granted much of the time sleep is innocent. A chance to regenerate one' body and recharge one' mind. In quiet sleep we recover from the chaos of life.

## II. Key Word: health

**1. As the thematic word of this chapter, *health* is always referred to in our daily spoken and written discourse under today's health-conscious circumstances, therefore it is of great significance to collect some "health"-related expressions in order to better voice your health concern and health proposal. Please summarize the useful expressions from the excerpt of the corpus.**

| | | |
|---|---|---|
| t treatment and restored his mental | **health** | ./We can at least be thankfu |
| most effective for preserving their | **health** | ." We have the tools to answer t |
| rients that are necessary for good | **health** | . If people want to be healthy an |
| rsonal decisions that may concern our | **health** | . If we so desire , we can smoke |
| a pet . All of us want to enjoy good | **health** | . Thousands of articles are writte   5 |
| " True friendship is like sound | **health** | ; the value of it is seldom known |
| n gas-powered cars to extraordinary | **health** | advances , John Ingham reports |

| | | |
|---|---|---|
| urces , declining energy and failing | health | against the growing demands of |
| te to have a wife who , despite ill | health | and children to look after , cook |
| any participants told of losing their | health | and life insurance . But that was    10 |
| — and someone who is in excellent | health | and pays attention to the body 's |
| cal change that directly threatens the | health | and safety of people is an enviro |
| ecessary to be careful in preserving | health | by due exercise and great tempe |
| ng overworked ./A lack of regular | health | checks and an unhealthy lifestyle |
| and great strides toward achieving " | health | for all by the year 2000 " ( a maj    15 |
| as a domestic was small and her frail | health | often kept her from working at a |
| om . Many of our residents had severe | health | or personality problems , or mentall |
| have the kind of robust and bountiful | health | that 's expected to be the norm |
| percent . Relaxation produces better | health | through deep , rhythmic breathin |
| boarding school your mum ruined her | health | to pay for . Then at Cambridge you    20 |
| ago . Morelli was 28 and in perfect | health | when she met with an insurance |
| e breast but it can also damage your | health | when you are at the wheel . Rec |

_____

_____

_____

_____

_____

_____

_____

_____

**2. Please translate the following Chinese sentences into English, trying to use the collocations and expressions from the above concordance lines.**

1) 吸烟、酗酒、熬夜等不良生活习惯将会无法挽回地损害我们的健康。

_____

2) 新鲜的空气、适度的运动、合理的饮食和充足的睡眠将有助于我们保持身体健康。

_____

3) 对从精神抑郁到心脏病的一系列疾病的研究显示，社会关系的存在能帮助人们抵御疾病的侵袭，相反这种支持的缺失却可能使健康亮红灯。

_____

4) 健康的身体是我们最稳固的地基，在它之上才有可能建造人生的摩天大楼。

_____

**3. Please appreciate the following excerpts from the corpus.**

1) The same listlessness, I am afraid, characterizes the use of all our faculties and senses. Only the deaf appreciate hearing, only the blind realize the blessings that lie in sight. Particularly does this observation apply to those who lost sight and hearing in adult life. But those who have never suffered loss of sight or hearing damage seldom make the fullest use of these blessed faculties. Their eyes and ears take in all sights and sounds hazily, without concentration, and with little appreciation. It is the same old story of not being grateful for what we have until we lose it, of not being conscious of health until we are ill.

2) This father and mother have two different ways of looking at the world. Whenever something bad happens to him—a call from the bank manager, a disagreement with his wife, even a frown from his employer—he imagines the worst: bankruptcy, jail, divorce, and dismissal. He is prone to depression; he often feels extremely tired; his health suffers. She, on the other hand, sees bad events in their least threatening light. To her, they are temporary challenges to be overcome. After a reversal, she bounces back quickly, and finds all her energy again. Her health is excellent.

3) Most of us take life for granted. We know that one day we must die, but usually we picture that day as far in the future. When we are in good health, death is all but unimaginable. We seldom think of it. The days stretch out endlessly. So we go about petty tasks, hardly aware of our listless attitude towards life.

# The Wonders of Nature

**Warming up**

We endearingly call her Mother Nature, because we humans, and all other beings, are all her products. She presents myriads of wonderful objects to us, which become meaningful, as Emerson puts it, only "when the mind is open to their influence."

Read the three texts below carefully and think how our minds (and bodies as well) can be influenced by nature.

## Text A

### Nature (excerpted)

By Ralph Waldo Emerson

**A Critical Reader (I)**

1. To go into solitude[1], a man needs to retire as much from his chamber as from society. I am not solitary whilst I read and write, though nobody is with me. But if a man would be alone, let him look at the stars. The rays that come from those heavenly worlds, will separate between him and what he touches. One might think the atmosphere was made transparent with this design, to give man, in the heavenly bodies, the perpetual presence of the sublime. Seen in the streets of cities, how great they are! If the stars should appear one night in a thousand years, how would men believe and adore; and preserve for many generations the remembrance of the city of God which had been shown! But every night come out these envoys of beauty, and light the universe with their admonishing smile.

2. The stars awaken a certain reverence, because though always present, they are inaccessible; but all natural objects make a kindred impression, when the mind is open to their influence. Nature never wears a

1 What does Emerson suggest one should do when one wants to go into solitude?
2 Why?

3 How should we treat natural objects?

mean appearance. Neither does the wisest man extort her secret, and lose his curiosity by finding out all her perfection. Nature never became a toy to a wise spirit. The flowers, the animals, the mountains, reflected the wisdom of his best hour, as much as they had delighted the simplicity of his childhood. When we speak of nature in this manner, we have a distinct but most poetical sense in the mind. We mean the integrity of impression made by manifold natural objects. It is this which distinguishes the stick of timber of the wood-cutter, from the tree of the poet. The charming landscape which I saw this morning, is indubitably[2] made up of some twenty or thirty farms. Miller owns this field, Locke that, and Manning the woodland beyond. But none of them owns the landscape. There is a property in the horizon which no man has but he whose eye can integrate all the parts, that is, the poet. This is the best part of these men's farms, yet to this their warranty-deeds[3] give no title[4]. To speak truly, few adult persons can see nature. Most persons do not see the sun. At least they have a very superficial seeing. The sun illuminates only the eye of the man, but shines into the eye and the heart of the child. The lover of nature is he whose inward and outward senses are still truly adjusted to each other; who has retained the spirit of infancy even into the era of manhood. His intercourse with heaven and earth, becomes part of his daily food. In the presence of nature, a wild delight runs through the man, in spite of real sorrows.

3. Nature says, —he is my creature, and maugre[5] all his impertinent griefs, he shall be glad with me. Not the sun or the summer alone, but every hour and season yields its tribute of delight; for every hour and change corresponds to and authorizes a different state of the mind, from breathless noon to grimmest midnight. Nature is a setting that fits equally well a comic or a mourning piece. In good health, the air is a cordial[6] of incredible virtue. Crossing a bare common[7], in snow puddles, at twilight, under a clouded sky, without having in my thoughts any occurrence of special good fortune, I have enjoyed a perfect exhilaration. I am glad to the brink of fear. In the woods too, a man casts off his years, as the snake his slough[8], and at what period soever

4 What differences do you see between the timber stick of the wood-cutter and the tree of the poet?

5 Why does the author say the charming landscape gives no title to the farm owners?

6 What kind of person is a true lover of nature?

7 What are included in Emerson's list of optimistic views of nature?

8 How does Emerson feel when he gets close to nature in the woods?

of life, is always a child. In the woods, is perpetual youth. Within these plantations of God, a decorum[9] and sanctity[10] reign, a perennial[11] festival is dressed, and the guest sees not how he should tire of them in a thousand years. In the woods, we return to reason and faith. There I feel that nothing can befall[12] me in life, —no disgrace, no calamity, (leaving me my eyes,) which nature cannot repair. Standing on the bare ground, —my head bathed by the blithe[13] air, and uplifted into infinite space, —all mean egotism[14] vanishes. I become a transparent eye-ball; I am nothing; I see all; the currents of the Universal Being circulate through me; I am part or particle of God. The name of the nearest friend sounds then foreign and accidental: to be brothers, to be acquaintances, —master or servant, is then a trifle and a disturbance. I am the lover of uncontained and immortal beauty. In the wilderness, I find something more dear and connate[15] than in streets or villages. In the tranquil[16] landscape, and especially in the distant line of the horizon, man beholds somewhat as beautiful as his own nature.

4. The greatest delight which the fields and woods minister, is the suggestion of an occult relation between man and the vegetable. I am not alone and unacknowledged. They nod to me, and I to them. The waving of the boughs in the storm, is new to me and old. It takes me by surprise, and yet is not unknown. Its effect is like that of a higher thought or a better emotion coming over me, when I deemed I was thinking justly or doing right.

5. Yet it is certain that the power to produce this delight, does not reside in nature, but in man, or in a harmony of both. It is necessary to use these pleasures with great temperance[17]. For, nature is not always tricked in holiday attire, but the same scene which yesterday breathed perfume and glittered as for the frolic of the nymphs, is overspread with melancholy today. Nature always wears the colors of the spirit. To a man laboring under calamity, the heat of his own fire hath sadness in it. Then, there is a kind of contempt of the landscape felt by him who has just lost by death a dear friend. The sky is less grand as it shuts down over less worth in the population.

[9] Why does Emerson not feel alone and unacknowledged in the fields and woods?

[10] What does Emerson think produces all the delight he gets from nature?

## Notes

1. solitude /'sɔlitjuːd/ *n.*  the state of being alone, undisturbed, or lonely. solitary /'sɔlitəri/ *adj.*
2. indubitably /in'duːbitəbli/ *adv.*  undoubtedly
3. warranty-deeds  a deed that binds a seller of property to defend the security of the title against any claims that may arise against the buyer (全权证书)
4. give no title to sb./give sb. no title  give sb. no right to possess (property)
5. maugre /'mɔːgə/ *prep.*  despite, in spite of
6. cordial /'kɔːdjəl/ *n.*  strong highly flavored sweet liquor usually drunk after a meal. *adj.* warm and friendly
7. common /'kɔmən/ *n.*  a piece of open land for recreational use in an urban area
8. slough /sluː, slaʊ/ *n.*  the cast-off skin of a snake
9. decorum /di'kɔːrəm/ *n.*  propriety in manners and conduct
10. sanctity /'sæŋktiti/ *n.*  the quality of being holy
11. perennial /pə'reniːəl/ *adj.*  lasting an indefinitely long time; suggesting self-renewal
12. befall /bi'fɔːl/ *v.*  (usu. sth. bad) happen to sb.
13. blithe /blaiθ/ *adj.*  carefree and happy and lighthearted
14. egotism /'iːgətiz(ə)m/ *n.*  an exaggerated opinion of one's own importance; an inflated feeling of pride in one's superiority to others
15. connate /'kɔneit/ *adj.*  related in nature
16. tranquil /'træŋkwil/ *adj.*  calm, free from disturbance
17. temperance /'tempərəns/ *n.*  the trait of avoiding excesses

## A Critical Reader (II)

1. Emerson talks about the importance of integrating all parts of nature. Suppose you are going to have an outing into the countryside, how can you better enjoy the beauty of the landscape following Emerson's advice?

2. Emerson says, "…the power to produce this delight, does not reside in nature, but in man, or in a harmony of both." What do you think we should do in order to achieve harmony between man and nature?

# A Critical Writer

## I. Basic Writing Techniques

### 1. Style and word choice

Text A is taken from Nature, an essay by Ralph Waldo Emerson, a 19th-century American essayist and poet, in which he expresses his _____ (A. indifference to  B. delight in  C. fear of) nature. The excerpt is written in the style of (A. lyrical prose  B. academic writing  C. narrative description), which is noticeably marked by the author's (A. descriptions of facts  B. ways of telling a story  C. expressive outlets of emotions).

**1.1** The following are emotion words used in Text A. Please put them into different groups.

| delight | alone | glad | adore | befall | blithe | contempt |
| disturbance | egotism | emotion | enjoy | exhilaration | fear | feel |
| grief | grim | harmony | melancholy | mourning | pleasures | reverence |
| sadness | solitary | solitude | sorrow | tranquil | | |

1) Gladness

_____  _____  _____  _____  _____  _____

2) Sadness

_____  _____  _____  _____  _____  _____

3) Peace and quiet

_____  _____  _____  _____  _____  _____

4) Love

_____  _____  _____  _____  _____  _____

5) Other emotions (Identify what.)

_____  _____  _____  _____  _____  _____

**1.2** To arouse the reader's emotions, the lyrical prose writer composes sentences in poetical language. When we read Text A, we should pay special attention to how such sentences are made. Make sentences by following the models taken from the text and by translating the Chinese given.

1) The flowers, the animals, the mountains, reflected the wisdom of his best hour, as much as they had delighted the simplicity of his childhood.

朝霞反映出青春的活力，就像晚霞代表着老年最后的灿烂。

_____

_____

2) In the presence of nature, a wild delight runs through the man, in spite of real sorrows.

面对大火，一阵冰冷的恐惧感传遍了我的全身，尽管大火的热浪就在身边。

_____

_____

3) In the wilderness, I find something more dear and connate than in streets or villages.

在阅读中，我发现了比在现实生活中更有趣、更令人激动的东西。

4) Standing on the bare ground, —my head bathed by the blithe air, and uplifted into infinite space, —all mean egotism vanishes.

看着人群向她挥手，全身沉浸在兴奋的氛围之中，一切恐惧一消而散。

5) The same scene which yesterday breathed perfume and glittered as for the frolic of the nymphs, is overspread with melancholy today.

昨天还吐芳露艳的花朵，今天却被笼罩在凄凉的孤寂之中。

## 2. Basic rules for good paragraphs and essays

### 2.1 Unity: one single topic.

As a lyrical prose, Text A contains sentences that sometimes may seem to be loosely related in each of the paragraphs. But actually, they all center around one single topic, that is, the harmony between man and nature.

Let's look at how each paragraph ends in Text A.

**Paragraph 1:** If the stars should appear one night in a thousand years, how would men believe and adore; and preserve for many generations the remembrance of the city of God which had been shown! But every night come out these envoys of beauty, and light the universe with their admonishing smile.

**Paragraph 2:** In the presence of nature, a wild delight runs through the man, in spite of real sorrows.

**Paragraph 3:** In the tranquil landscape, and especially in the distant line of the horizon, man beholds somewhat as beautiful as his own nature.

**Paragraph 4:** The waving of the boughs in the storm, is new to me and old. It takes me by surprise, and yet is not unknown. Its effect is like that of a higher thought or a better emotion coming over me, when I deemed I was thinking justly or doing right.

**Paragraph 5:** Nature always wears the colors of the spirit. To a man laboring under calamity, the heat of his own fire hath sadness in it. Then, there is a kind of contempt of the landscape felt by him who has just lost by death a dear friend. The sky is less grand as it shuts down over less worth in the population.

**Analysis:** From all these concluding sentences in the paragraphs, we can see very clearly the relationship or harmony between man and nature as the author sees it.

Please find other sentences that describe the relationship between man and nature in Text A.

### 2.2 Coherence: logical line of thoughts.

Sometimes the lyrical prose writer may let his emotions flow in such a free manner that it seems a little difficult to follow his emotional flowing. But still his line of thoughts is well controlled along a certain channel. Read the first paragraph carefully and see how the currents of emotions finally pour into the same aqueduct.

To go into solitude, a man needs to retire as much from his chamber as from society. I am not solitary whilst I read and write, though nobody is with me. But if a man would be alone, let him look at the stars. The rays that come from those heavenly worlds, will separate between him and what he touches. One might think the atmosphere was made transparent with this design, to give man, in the heavenly bodies, the perpetual presence of the sublime. Seen in the streets of cities, how great they are! If the stars should appear one night in a thousand years, how would men believe and adore; and preserve for many generations the remembrance of the city of God which had been shown! But every night come out these envoys of beauty, and light the universe with their admonishing smile. (Paragraph 1)

**Analysis:** The above paragraph follows the logical line of thoughts illustrated below:

Solitude → retiring from his chamber as well as from society → reading and writing (in his chamber)

Looking at the stars (as a way of retiring from his chamber) → rays from those heavenly worlds (stars) → separating him and what he touches

The transparent atmosphere → giving man perpetual presence of the sublime (stars) → greatness of the stars

Stars appearing one night in a thousand years → how would men preserve the remembrance → The envoys of beauty (stars) coming out every night and lighting the universe with their admonishing smile

All the above flows of thoughts are connected by the act of looking at the stars.

Please study the line of thoughts of Paragraph 2.

### 2.3　Cohesive devices: repetitions, substitutions and examples.

Examples, repetitions and substitutions are commonly used devices for cohesion.

**Analysis:** When the author talks about nature, he gives some examples to illustrate its beauty. For example, in the first two paragraphs, he mentions the stars and repeats the word stars several times. But in other cases, he uses other words to substitute stars such as:

*Heavenly worlds, heavenly bodies, the sublime, city of God, and envoys of beauty.*

Please find other examples showing the beauty of nature given in Text A.

## II. Specific Writing Techniques

### 1. Figures of speech—Metaphor and Personification

Figurative language, though also used in other types of writing, is especially common in lyrical writing. In Text A, Emerson uses quite a few figures of speech like ***metaphor, simile*** and ***personification***.

# Chapter Seven　The Wonders of Nature

**1.1　Read the sentences taken from the text and identify whether they are metaphors or personifications. Put an M for metaphor, an S for simile, a P for personification, or both an M/S and a P in cases where both figures of speech co-occur in the square after each sentence. Please explain what is compared to what or what is personified.**

1) But every night come out these envoys of beauty, and light the universe with their admonishing smile.

2) The stars awaken a certain reverence.

3) Neither does the wisest man extort her secret, and lose his curiosity by finding out all her perfection.

4) Nature says, —he is my creature, and maugre all his impertinent griefs, ….

5) In good health, the air is a cordial of incredible virtue.

6) In the woods too, a man casts off his years, as the snake his slough.

**1.2　Complete the following sentences in which metaphors or personifications are used.**

1) Love is a fruit, in season at all times and within the reach of every hand. Anyone may _____ it and no limit is set.
　　A) get　　　　B) take　　　　C) gather　　　D) catch

2) Love is no hot-house flower, but a wild _____, born of a wet night, born of an hour of sunshine; sprung from wild seed, blown along the road by a wild wind.
　　A) plant　　　B) crop　　　　C) life　　　　D) growth

3) Love is the rosy cloud in the morning of life; and if it does too often resolve itself into the _____, yet, to my mind, it only makes our nature more fruitful in what is excellent and amiable.
　　A) water　　　B) shower　　　C) vapor　　　D) dewdrops

4) They say love is a two-way street. But I don't believe it, because the one I've been on for the last two years was a dirt _____.
　　A) place　　　B) road　　　　C) spot　　　　D) house

5) Happiness is the china shop; love is the _____.
　　A) cat　　　　B) rat　　　　　C) bull　　　　D) pig

6) The wind sang her mournful _____ through the falling leaves.
　　A) sound　　　B) song　　　　C) voice　　　D) noise

7) The rain _____ my cheeks as it fell.
　　A) struck　　　B) washed　　　C) kissed　　　D) cleaned

8) The daffodils nodded their yellow _____ at the walkers.
　　A) stems　　　B) nectars　　　C) petals　　　D) heads

9) The car engine _____ and sputtered when it started during the blizzard.
　　A) coughed　　B) yelled　　　C) shouted　　　D) roared

10) The china _____ on the shelves during the earthquake.
　　A) danced　　　B) moved　　　C) sat　　　　D) lay

## 2. Negation

Negation sometimes gives greater force to the statement than affirmation. Read the *italicized* sentences below which are taken from the text, paying special attention to how negation is used.

Nature never wears a mean appearance. Neither does the wisest man extort her secret, and lose his curiosity by finding out all her perfection. Nature never became a toy to a wise spirit. The flowers, the animals, the mountains, reflected the wisdom of his best hour, as much as they had delighted the simplicity of his childhood. (Paragraph 2)

Rewrite the following sentences using negation without changing the meanings.

1) Within these plantations of God, I feel that nature can repair any disgrace, any calamity that befall me in life.
_____

2) Most persons see the sun very superficially.
_____

3) I am acknowledged and have company, because the vegetable nod to me, and I nod to them.
_____

4) The waving of the boughs in the storm is known to me, yet it still takes me by surprise.
_____

5) Every hour and season yields its tribute of delight.
_____

## III. Your Turn to Write

Read Paragraph 4 in Text A and write an essay of at least three paragraphs on the topic "Alone with Nature", following the outline below.

### Alone with Nature

1. In the bustling city, I oftentimes feel lonely.

2. Paradoxically, I can cure myself of this loneliness by staying alone with nature in the woods far away from the city.

3. The greatest delight which the woods minister, is from the company I find in all things around.

## Pearls of Wisdom

1. We mean the integrity of impression made by manifold natural objects. It is this which distinguishes the stick of timber of the wood-cutter, from the tree of the poet. —Ralph Waldo Emerson

2. Yet it is certain that the power to produce this delight, does not reside in nature, but in man, or in a harmony of both. —Ralph Waldo Emerson

3. I only went out for a walk and finally concluded to stay out till sundown, for going out, I found, was really going in. —John Muir

4. I love to think of nature as an unlimited broadcasting station, through which God speaks to us every hour, if we will only tune in.

—George Washington Carver

5. Forget not that the earth delights to feel your bare feet and the winds long to play with your hair. —Kahlil Gibran

## Text B

### Warming up

1 What do you like best about flowers?
2 What flowers do you like best? Can you name some?
3 What do the flowers you like symbolize?

### A Short Look at the Colorful World of Flowers

By Adriana Noton

**A Critical Reader (I)**

1. There are few things on this planet that bring more happiness, color, and beauty than flowers. The different kinds of joy they can bring to people are only exceeded by the number of its species, and that comes in literally by thousands. You do not have to be a botanist to appreciate the value of a flower; you need only have sense for the profound exquisiteness[1]. With this in mind, let's delve a bit deeper into the world of flowers.

1 Why do you like flowers?

2 What feelings do flowers usually give you?

2. Two categories of flower that you may be familiar with are the annual[2] and perennial[3]. The annual is one that comes and goes over the course of one season. That is to say, they sprout, flower, seed and ultimately die over the course of a growing season. Further, this type of flower can be broken down into summer and winter

3 To what categories does the author put flowers into?

annuals. Examples of annuals include both zinnias and marigolds.

3. A perennial on the other hand is a flower that lives for more than two years. Usually they are small flowering plants. They bloom in spring or summer, die in autumn or winter, then spring up again during the next growing season. These are referred to as herbaceous perennials and one example is the red clover.

4. One of the most famous and popular of all perennials is the tulip. It is a bulbous plant that can lay claim to many homes. They can be found from The Netherlands to Iran and from Turkey to northern China. They are cup-shaped flowers that can grow as long as two feet. They also come in a kaleidoscope of vibrant colors.

5. For many people roses come attached with the deepest of sentiments. They have been eternal symbols of love and beauty. Interestingly, one Biblical legend has it that the first rose was white but blushed red over the actions of Adam and Eve. Moreover, they are the national flower for both the United States and England.

6. Roses do not hold the patent on flower symbolism. Daisies are often thought of as reflective of innocence. Poppies are often given to those grieving the death of a loved one, especially those who have fallen during wartime. You will often see an iris being tossed upon a casket as its meaning for some connotes resurrection.

7. Flowers also have a practical side. They can be used for all sorts of things. Jasmine and chamomile have been infused into tea for a fragrant and medicinal beverage. All types are given as celebratory gifts, from christenings to social functions and holidays. They can even be used as a food, although they are not heavily marketed as such. However, sunflowers, chrysanthemums, and honeysuckle, to name but a few, are all edible. One popular drink made from a flower is dandelion wine.

8. One endearing quality about flowers is their accessibility. You can purchase them from your local florist, supermarket, or even online. But more than that, you can start your own garden, either on a patch of available land or even in a flower box. It doesn't take enormous resources to usher beauty into your life.

4 Where are the tulips usually found?

5 Think about the different things flowers symbolize.

6 What practical uses do flowers have?

7 What endearing quality does the author mean?

## Notes

1. exquisiteness /ɪkˈskwɪzɪtnɪs/ *n.*   extreme beauty
2. annual /ˈænjuəl/ *adv.*   completing its life cycle within a year. n. a plant that completes its entire life cycle within the space of a year
3. perennial /pəˈrɛniəl/ *adj.*   lasting three seasons or more. n. a plant lasting for three seasons or more

## A Critical Reader (II)

1. What flowers do you personally like best?
2. On different occasions such as a birthday, a ceremony, the Mothers' or the Fathers' Day, or house warming celebration, what flowers do you send your family or friends as gifts?
3. What do they symbolize?

## A Critical Writer

### I. Style and word choice

#### 1. Collocation

Very important in learning a language is collocation, which means words habitually go with certain other words. For instance, we usually say a ***tall tree***, but rarely a *\*high tree*, although tall and high are often considered synonymous. However, we can say a ***tall building*** or a ***high building***. There are two columns of words below. Join a word in Column A with one of the words in Column B if the two words collocate or properly go together. Sometimes a word in Column A may go with different words in Column B and vice versa.

| A | B |
|---|---|
| Celebratory | Colors |
| Deep | Exquisiteness |
| Eternal | Flowers |
| Enormous | Functions |
| Fragrant | Gifts |
| Perennial | Symbols |
| Practical | Plants |
| Profound | Purposes |
| Social | Resources |
| Vibrant | Sentiments |

## 2. Symbolism

In Text B, the author talks about what flowers symbolize. The following are the names of some flowers. Write a sentence about each of them to explain what it symbolizes. Try to use different sentence patterns. If the text never gives relevant information, consult reference books or go online for that information.

| | | |
|---|---|---|
| 1) chamomile | 甘菊 | |
| 2) chrysanthemum | 菊花 | |
| 3) red clover | 红三叶草 | |
| 4) daisy | 雏菊 | |
| 5) dandelion | 蒲公英 | |
| 6) honeysuckle | 金银花 | |
| 7) iris | 鸢尾花 | |
| 8) jasmine | 茉莉花 | |
| 9) marigold | 万寿菊；金盏花 | |
| 10) poppy | 罂粟（花） | |
| 11) rose | 玫瑰花 | |
| 12) sunflower | 向日葵 | |
| 13) zinnia | 鱼尾菊 | |

## II. Basic rules for good sentences and essays

### 1. Paraphrase the following sentences, using the expressions in the brackets.

1) Flowers bring the most happiness, color, and beauty on this planet. (more…than)

2) Feelings about this vary from person to person. (be only exceeded by)

3) It doesn't require a lot of math to work out the problem; it only requires some counting skill. (have to be)

4) They sell different products including radios, TV sets, calculators, computers, and so on. (from…to…)

5) They are not the only people to enjoy such advantages. (hold the patent on)

**2. Classification and definition**

Text B classifies flowers into two categories—the annual and the perennial flowers and gives definitions to them:

*Two categories of flower that you may be familiar with are the annual and perennial.*

*The annual is one that comes and goes over the course of one season.*

*A perennial on the other hand is a flower that lives for more than two years.*

We can also use some other verbs and/or nouns to do the classification and definition:

*Flowers <u>are divided into</u> two <u>groups</u>.*

*There are two <u>types</u> of flowers—the annual and the perennial.*

*The annual flowers <u>refer to</u> those that come and go over the course of one season.*

*Flowers that live for more than two years <u>are called</u> / <u>are known as</u> perennial flowers.*

The following are a list of words used to classify or define:

| Classification | | Definition | |
| --- | --- | --- | --- |
| Verb | Noun | Verb | Noun |
| classify | class | be | definition |
| categorize | category | refer to | |
| divide into | group | be called | |
| put into | type | be known as | |
| there are | kind | Mean | |
| break down into | | | |

Please write some sentences to classify things and give a definition to each classification.

## III. Your Turn to Write

Read Paragraphs 2 and 3 in Text B and rewrite them, changing the ways flowers are classified and defined.

## Pearls of Wisdom

1. You do not have to be a botanist to appreciate the value of a flower; you need only have sense for the profound exquisiteness. —Adriana Noton
2. It doesn't take enormous resources to usher beauty into your life.
—Adriana Noton
3. Earth laughs in flowers. —Ralph Waldo Emerson
4. I perhaps owe having become a painter to flowers. —Claude Monet
5. Bread feeds the body, indeed, but flowers feed also the soul. —The Koran

# Text C

## Unsolved Mystery—the Sea

By Peter Freuchen

1. I read about the seven seas in Greenland, although I was born and raised in a little port in Denmark. I had known ships and sailors and stories about famous voyages all my life, but when I sat through the long, dark nights of the arctic winters at Thule[1] for years, I discovered the wondrous ocean in my imagination.

2. There was little enough of it that we could see, for all winter long the ice stretched out for interminable miles in front of us, firm and solid. As soon as the sun showed over the horizon in spring, we had a wide outlook; but it took months for the ice to break up, and during that time it was tantalizing to look out from the shore at huge icebergs drifting south in endless procession. In my mind I followed those big fragments of icecap as they floated eternally to their doom. I thought of them sailing so majestically south until they were off Newfoundland[2]; I knew they would turn east there and meet the warm waters of the Gulf Stream where they would die, swiftly and inevitably, for the Gulf Stream can finish off even a large berg in twenty-four hours.

3. Well, I wondered, where does the Gulf Stream originate, and why band how does it happen to be exactly where it is? On the sail of my imagination still, I followed this mighty current to where it is born in the Caribbean.

### A Critical Reader

**1** Why does the author say he discovered the wondrous ocean in his imagination?

**2** What did he see in his imagination of the sea?

**3** How does the author lead the reader to his main topic—unsolved mysteries of the sea?

Chapter Seven  The Wonders of Nature  45

That took me to the waters of other currents, and to studying the winds and tides that play such an important part in the mysterious movements of the sea. Why, I asked myself, do the winds blow so steadily in one place and so capriciously in another, and not at all somewhere else; why should the tide rise as high as a house on one coast and hardly at all on another? Why twice a day in most of the world, but in some places only once? And where, after all, does that water come from in the first place?

4. Little by little it dawned upon me that there is a logical connection between all the things that happen in that immense connected body of salted water that covers 71 per cent of the surface of the earth. There is, indeed, a grant pattern in the wonderful phenomena of the ocean. This pattern regulates the ocean's storms and calms, deeps and shallows, the animals and plants that inhabit it, the birds flying over it, its islands, volcanoes, and caves, and even the men and ships moving about on its surface.

5. Since those long, dark, lonely winters in Thule, I never have stopped wondering and learning about the seven seas[3]. Why seven? This was one of the first questions I asked myself, since I could easily name seven times seven that are called seas on the maps. For every answer I found, there were two new questions, because the majesty and mystery of the sea are inexhaustible, and much lies beyond the comprehension of man. Man feels himself weak and impotent when he faces its might, for no one can halt the tides or fight the currents or control the waves. But everywhere men feel a compulsion to pit their strength against the sea, to explore it and wander about on it, to use it for their own ends and wrest its wealth from it.

6. Primitive people worshipped the sea out of fear of what it might do to them, and in gratitude for the treasures which it washed up for them on its beaches. The Romans believed the sea to be a dark kingdom ruled by a god whom they called Neptune. Today we know a great deal more than was known in ancient times; yet we still stand on the shore, humble in our insignificance as we face the waves rolling in from a turbulent ocean.

7. When gales whip the trees and rattle our windows, or snow piles up outside so that no one wants to go for a walk, landlubbers snug and safe in a warm room

[4] What important point did he gradually realize?
[5] What is the logical connection between all the things that happen in the ocean?

[6] What do you know about the seven seas? What are they?

[7] What did primitive people think of the sea?
[8] How would you feel when you stand on the shore looking out into the sea?

are likely to tell each other how sorry they feel for all the poor sailors on a night like this. But underneath the sympathetic talk, they actually feel a little wistful envy of the men who brave the winds, rain, snow, cold, and storms upon the restless water. Then on a fine day the sight of foreign seamen, or of tall ships from far away, or of an exotic bit of merchandise from halfway round the world gives us a pang of jealousy of the men who move about over the sea viewing the wonders of the deep. And it must be confessed that these incredible wonders lose nothing in the seamen's telling of them, for their words seem to set fire to the imagination and give shore-bound people a sense of excitement that they can never find on land.

8. The fascinating stories these fellows bring us are the stuff our dreams are made of. In these dreams, we experience countless exciting adventures, baffling the most violent storms, conquering the bravest fighters, foiling the most bloodthirsty pirates, bringing home the richest cargoes, diving for sunken gold, and seeing the strangest sights. Then, in the end, scientists take over from imagination—and behold, there are even greater wonders than we dreamed.

From *Book of the Seven Seas*, Julian Messner, Inc.

**9** Under the surface of their sympathy, how do shore-bound people actually feel about the sailors in bad weather?

**10** What do you think the author might talk about in paragraphs following the text C?

### Notes

1. Thule /'θjuːliː/ *n.*   a town in northwestern Greenland, belonging to Denmark
2. Newfoundland /ˌnjuːfənd'lænd/ *n.*   a large island in the north Atlantic, belonging to Canada
3. the seven seas   all the seas and oceans in the world, but historically they refer to different sets of seven seas known to ancient people

## A Critical Writer

### I. Paraphrasing

Rewrite the following sentences using the phrases in the brackets.

1) The thick layers of frozen snow and ice sealed up the mountain village. The people patiently stayed indoors in the long, boring winter until it was over. (sit through)

2) Gradually I realized that all things in the world are somehow related to each other. (dawn on/upon)

3) Man does not understand very well the majesty and mystery of the universe. (beyond the comprehension)

4) Although we talk about them sympathetically, we actually feel a little envy of the sailors. (underneath the sympathetic talk)

5) When we see an exotic bit of merchandise from halfway round the world, we feel a pang of jealousy of the seamen who can enjoy viewing the wonders of the deep. (the sight of)

## II. The Smooth Stream of Ideas

A text should run smoothly from sentence to sentence and from paragraph to paragraph. Let's take a look at how the last sentence in Paragraph 1 and the first in Paragraph 2 are logically linked.

..., I discovered the wondrous ocean.

There was little enough of it that we could see, for all winter long the ice stretched out for interminable miles in front of us, firm and solid.

What is said in each of the clauses is explained by the following clause:

Why did I discover the wondrous ocean only in my imagination? ← Little enough of the ocean we could see;

Why could we see little enough? ← Ice covered large stretches of the ocean.

Write two small paragraphs by following the logical stream of ideas shown below, mentioning your failure to come to office in the last sentence of the first paragraph. You should write several other sentences before coming to the failure.

failure to come to office ← road damaged ← traffic closed ← landslide ← heavy downpour

**Paragraph 1**: _____
_____
_____
_____

**Paragraph 2**: _____
_____
_____
_____

## Pearls of Wisdom

1. Man feels himself weak and impotent when he faces its might, for no one can halt the tides or fight the currents or control the waves. —Peter Freuchen

2. The sea pronounces something, over and over, in a hoarse whisper; I cannot quite make it out. —Annie Dillard

3. Never a ship sails out of the bay / But carries my heart as a stowaway.
   —Roselle Mercier Montgomery

4. Praise the sea; on shore remain. —John Florio

# Corpus-based Exercises (7)

## I. Key Word: nature

Compare the following two groups of concordance lines. Group A show all instances of *nature* used in Text A. In all instances in Group A, *nature* refers to the natural world except in Line 11, where the word means the same as *nature* is used in lines in Group B, indicating an essential quality or characteristic of a person or thing. What differences do you see between the uses of *nature* in these two meanings?

Group A:

| | | |
|---|---|---|
| pression, when the mind is open to their influence. | **Nature** | never wears a mean appearance. Neither |
| lose his curiosity by finding out all her perfection. | **Nature** | never became a toy to a wise spirit. The |
| d the simplicity of his childhood. When we speak of | **nature** | in this manner, we have a distinct but mo |
| e no title. To speak truly, few adult persons can see | **nature** | . Most persons do not see the sun. At least |
| into the eye and the heart of the child. The lover of | **nature** | is he whose inward and outward senses are  5 |
| , becomes part of his daily food. In the presence of | **nature** | , a wild delight runs through the man, in s |
| runs through the man, in spite of real sorrows. / | **Nature** | says, —he is my creature, and maugre all |
| mind, from breathless noon to grimmest midnight. | **Nature** | is a setting that fits equally well a comic or |
| sgrace, no calamity, ( leaving me my eyes, ) which | **nature** | cannot repair. Standing on the bare ground    10 |
| rizon, man beholds somewhat as beautiful as his own | **nature** | . / The greatest delight which the fields |
| the power to produce this delight, does not reside in | **nature** | , but in man, or in a harmony of both. It is |
| ry to use these pleasures with great temperance. For, | **nature** | is not always tricked in holiday attire, but |
| of the nymphs, is overspread with melancholy today. | **Nature** | always wears the colors of the spirit. To a   15 |

Group B:

| | | |
|---|---|---|
| ternoons. Ben Franklin's use of a kite to explore the | **nature** | of lightning is just one example. In Scotla |

| | | |
|---|---|---|
| istmas , is symbolic of her human warmth , her giving | **nature** | , her noble character , and her high Christi |
| isplaced . Intelligence is just as much a part of human | **nature** | as friendliness . It would certainly be unna |
| ild and on the other with a world of complex physical | **nature** | . In a mood of self-defeat , they exclaim , " |
| , mostly , with each other 's assumptions about human | **nature** | , social relationships , and so on . / One of 5 |
| t he had a greater understanding of people and human | **nature** | than anyone who had ever lived . The results |
| ll skills require constant repetition to become second | **nature** | ; good manners are no exception . / One sim |

## II. Key Word: solitude

*Solitude* refers to a state of being alone with no one else around. Sometimes it has a good, positive connotation, and at other times the connotation is bad or negative. Study the following concordance lines and decide in which lines solitude sounds positive and in which it is used with negative connotation.

| | | |
|---|---|---|
| d that night too , and a very important one at that — | **solitude** | had ceased to be a precondition for his cre |
| n , is solitude , " he wrote . / No doubt about it , | **solitude** | is improved by being voluntary . / Look a |
| alarmed . This violation of concentration , silence , | **solitude** | goes to the very heart of our notion of lit |
| ed my time in order to produce change and growth . | **Solitude** | , isolation , or new environments in them |
| people , their temporary absence can be refreshing . | **Solitude** | will end on Thursday . If today I use a si 5 |
| here is no aspiration in hunger . Only shame . And | **solitude** | . Hunger creates its own prison walls ; |
| lt to endure without her mate . With loneliness and | **solitude** | , that tragedy has become her fate . Then , |
| g precious from the natural world—the peace and | **solitude** | these mammals once experienced . I fear t |
| found the companion that was so companionable as | **solitude** | . " / Thoreau had his own self-importance f |
| fference . It is a reliable and tireless buffer between | **solitude** | and loneliness , and for this it is often regar 10 |
| a couple of special qualities . One is a tolerance for | **solitude** | . Because we are so busy and on such a tig |
| odest and humble we feel , the more we suffer from | **solitude** | , feeling ourselves inadequate company . / |
| out an empty compartment , it seemed likely that his | **solitude** | wouldn't last for ever . In all honesty , ho |
| ff at one stroke : you are once more in the deaf , hot | **solitude** | of trembling air , alone in the cornfields . / |
| rn . And instantly they stand together in an immense | **solitude** | . / Lovers seek for privacy . Friends find thi 15 |
| . Now , that 's character for you . / Inspiration in | **solitude** | is a major commodity for poets and philos |
| people , most of the time , listen to their radios in | **solitude** | . Radio , then , is usually more than just a |
| had got into the habit of only doing creative work in | **solitude** | . / Even before he started going to school , |
| he was no longer able to concentrate on his work in | **solitude** | either . That day , when once again he end |
| To go into | **solitude** | , a man needs to retire as much from his c 20 |
| ers all by himself . " How graceful , how benign , is | **solitude** | , " he wrote . / No doubt about it , solitude |
| till they came home . / The American high priest of | **solitude** | was Thoreau . We admire him , not for his |
| ldom at the roadside , but far within the fields . The | **solitude** | and silence are deep and wide . Then , wh |
| en you can read . Get up early in the morning in the | **solitude** | that is only possible when other persons d |
| tude . / Lovers seek for privacy . Friends find this | **solitude** | about them , this barrier between them an 25 |

Positive (Line numbers): _____
Negative (Line numbers): _____
Hard to say (Line numbers): _____

## III. Key Word: symbol

**Study the *symbol* expressions from the concordance lines carefully and translate the Chinese sentences below them.**

| | | |
|---|---|---|
| y force or that guard company . / The lock is the new | **symbol** | of America . Indeed , a recent public-s |
| ave so many in Sweden , and which are for me the very | **symbol** | of an inhuman capitalism . / And given |
| of preconditioning and accepted the beige raincoat as a | **symbol** | of authority and status while they reject |
| surprised because in our culture a lily is regarded as a | **symbol** | of death . Husbands here might feel hu |
| increasingly expensive clothes , rapidly evolved into a | **symbol** | of fashion . Publishers paid huge sums   5 |
| ck it up . It was a blue book , the dreadful , chilling | **symbol** | of finals week . A blue book that some |
| akes Monsieur Verdoux , the French wife killer , into a | **symbol** | of hatred for women . / It 's a relief to |
| etter clothes can be produced by technology . Just as a | **symbol** | of my philosophy , I never use anything |
| Green representing Oceania / The Olympic flag is a | **symbol** | of peace , goodwill , and global solidar |
| enough to eat . In some religious groups , wealth was a | **symbol** | of probable salvation and high morals ,   10 |
| y , of style , of beauty . All over the world she was a | **symbol** | of selfless humanity , a standard-bearer |
| y believe that for many people , money is an important | **symbol** | of strength and influence . Husbands who |
| s northeast of Nairobi , Ms . Mbogo suddenly became a | **symbol** | of the growing powerful political force |
| eed , NASA describes the space station as " a powerful | **symbol** | of U . S . leadership " . |
| s , they managed to make a profit . Appropriately , the | **symbol** | of victory in the Olympic games is no l   15 |
| s take for granted . Lacking the culturally acceptable | **symbols** | of belonging in this setting , we becam |
| of as representing trickery , would make equally good | **symbols** | of devotion , since they also form lasti |
| he " right " clothes , eat the " right " foods . These | **symbols** | of distinction assure us and others that |
| ith the deepest of sentiments . They have been eternal | **symbols** | of love and beauty . Interestingly , one |
| each other . Geese , swans and mandarin ducks are all | **symbols** | of marital faithfulness ; field biologists   20 |
| ty that results from losing all our familiar signs and | **symbols** | of social intercourse , These signs or c |
| theaters , count votes or teach history . / The old | **symbols** | of technology are even more misleading |

1. 城市上空的蓝天白云可以被看作环保成就的标志。

_____

2. 神九任务的圆满完成标志着中国在宇宙探索中的胜利和一个新阶段的开始。

_____

3. 中秋的圆月代表着合家团圆，所以人们把中秋节当成思家的日子。

_____

4. 春天，地上的青草、树枝上的嫩芽、鸟儿和昆虫的鸣叫，代表着生命的复苏。

_____

5. 奥运会虽然是一个充满竞技的聚会，但正如奥运旗帜一样，也象征着和平、善意和宽容。

_____

## IV. Key Word: imagination

In Text C, the author talks about the seas with a lot of *imagination*. In fact, he uses the word *imagination* several times.

I discovered the wondrous ocean *in my imagination*.

*On the sail of my imagination* still, I followed this mighty current to where it is born in the Caribbean.

… their words seem to *set fire to the imagination* and give shore-bound people a sense of excitement ….

Then, in the end, scientists *take over from imagination* …, there are even greater wonders than we dreamed.

Below are concordance lines of *imagination* taken from a corpus of college English texts. Study the concordance lines carefully and then translate the Chinese sentences into English using collocations of *imagination* you learn from Text C and the concordance lines.

| | | | |
|---|---|---|---|
| . Creative people alternate between | imagination | and a deeply-rooted sense of reality . Great | |
| of money as a product of the creative | imagination | . The banker no longer offers us a safe : he | |
| reveled in feeling , had let my crude | imagination | roam , but the impulse to dream had been slow | |
| land . ' You 're letting your foolish | imagination | carry you away , Peigi daughter of Finlay , ' | |
| still at a loss to separate truth from | imagination | . / One quasi bag lady spends about eight hou | 5 |
| screen . / But that shock roused his | imagination | . Chaplin didn't have his jokes written into | |
| r scripts I 'm seeing everything in my | imagination | . I write quickly . I go like the wind . | |
| The flames of a wood fire stimulate my | imagination | " . By the end of the week , each twin has an | |
| he world for whom they were an item of | imagination | . It was not my first struggle with the disap | |
| rt and great science involve a leap of | imagination | into a world that is different from the prese | 10 |
| -minute " vacation " into the realm of | imagination | each day , you may add much to the excitement | |
| be limited by the boundaries of personal | imagination | . She said . " Because in this country , wher | |
| with Ivory that their numbers beat the | imagination | . Not even Proctor & Gamble knows how many | |
| Christa McAuliffe , who captured the | imagination | of the entire nation ; inspiring us with her | |
| long thought impossible—caught the | imagination | of everyone . The laboratory process that pro | 15 |
| th . He said that this exercise of the | imagination | left memory traces in his mind that would lat | |
| ent of success beyond the reach of the | imagination | . In this they probably owed much to their re | |
| work of art , Athenians prepare their | imagination | through learning and experience . To a Visigo | |
| ties where the students must use their | imagination | . For example , instead of simply asking WHEN | |
| and proved that I am beginning to use | imagination | to transform the actual incident . I was scar | 20 |
| the tale of a little girl with a wild | imagination | taking her first music lesson . I had turned | |

| | | |
|---|---|---|
| ur feet . Meeting rooms that free your | **imagination** | by opening to grand panoramas . And lobbies t |
| bed . Close your eyes , to permit your | **imagination** | to soar more freely . Many people find that t |
| w out questions . Challenge the kids ' | **imaginations** | . ' What might the earth be like if dinosaurs |
| fiction writers have used their human | **imaginations** | . This gives the writers some enormous advant |
| take it to the farthermost corners of our | **imaginations** | . Only knowledgeable people can wisely decide |
| hrough honesty and hard work fired the | **imaginations** | of many European readers : in Letters from an |

**The following list of *imagination* collocations is drawn from the above concordance lines.**

| | |
|---|---|
| alternate between imagination and reality | a leap of imagination into |
| be limited by the boundaries of imagination | a person with a wild imagination |
| beat one's imagination | a product of the imagination |
| capture one's imagination | an item of imagination |
| catch sb's imagination | the exercise of the imagination |
| challenge one's imagination | |
| fire sb's imagination | |
| free one's imagination | beyond the reach of the imagination |
| let one's foolish imagination carry one away | in one's imagination |
| let one's imagination roam | the realm of imagination |
| permit one's imagination to soar | |
| prepare one's imagination through doing something | |
| rouse sb's imagination | |
| separate truth from imagination | |
| stimulate one's imagination | |
| take sth. to the farthermost corners of one's imagination | |
| use one's imagination | |

1. 你简直是在痴人说梦，想入非非！
_____

2. 科幻小说曾点燃了很多科学家对大自然想象的火焰。
_____

3. 扬起想象的风帆，我们眼望着那艘轮船，直到它从天际渐渐地消失。
_____

4. 山顶上绮丽的景色引起了所有游客无限的遐想。
_____

5. 宇宙如此浩渺博大，远远超出了人类的想象。
_____

6. 在大自然中什么事情都会发生，只有想象不到的，没有不可能的。
_____

7. 仰望繁星点点的夜空，他在想象中与外星智能生物进行交流。
_____

8. 他有时过分富于想象，分不开现实和假想。
_____

# Entertainment

> **Warming up**
>
> The road to success in the circle of entertainment is unimaginably rough, which sounds contradictory to the spirit of entertainment. How do you understand this paradox?

## Text A

### Old Blue Eyes: A Look at the Life of Frank Sinatra

By All Music Matters

**A Critical Reader (I)**

1. Arguably the most important figure in popular music of the 20th century, Frank Sinatra is unquestionably an American Icon for the ages. Singing and promoting the American song as it was written, Sinatra consistently took the "standards" of great composers and reinterpreted them in such a way as to establish them as classics in their own right[1]. Despite countless changes in the times and popular tastes, he sustained a career spanning over 60 years and is revered still today.

① Can you offer at least one figure who weighs the same weight in the 21st century as Frank Sinatra did in the entertainment industry?

2. Born in Hoboken, New Jersey in 1915 to Sicilian[2]-American parents, Sinatra was an only child with little interest in school and proved so by dropping out to pursue music. Growing up in the swing era of the 1930's, he got his first break in 1935 when his mother persuaded a local trio[3], The Three Flashes, to accept him and become The Hoboken Four. Appearing on the radio show *Major Bowes Amateur Hour* and winning a 6 month touring gig with the program, <u>Sinatra was on his way</u>.

② What does the underlined part in Paragraph 2 mean?

3. Noticed by previous Benny Goodman trumpeter Harry James, Sinatra seized the opportunity to sign up and contribute vocals to 16 Top Ten hits and appear in two films with successful bandleader Tommy Dorsey by

1942. In the same year he recorded his first solo effort and Cole Porter's *Night and Day* become the first of what was to be countless chart entries under his own name. With influences like Bing Crosby[4], Billie Holiday[5] and Mabel Mercer[6], Sinatra was establishing his own sound that melded vocal jazz with upbeat swing and ballads.

4. Now in his mid twenties he had become the first real teen idol revealing a whole new audience for pop music, the "bobby soxers". Music, which had previously been recorded mainly for adults, was reaching a younger crowd. With four more Top Ten hits in 1943, including *People Will Say We're in Love* from the musical *Oklahoma!*, Sinatra was hired by the popular radio series *Your Hit Parade* and later a string of others including *The Frank Sinatra Show*.

5. During this time, Sinatra was lending himself to films increasingly as well and impressed MGM[7] enough to be signed to a contract. 1945's *Anchors Aweigh* with Gene Kelly[8] even went on to be the year's most successful film. The same year saw him with 8 Top Ten hits and another 8 in the following year (including the two #1's, *Oh! What It Seemed to Be* and *Five Minutes More*). Continuing in this vein[9], the singer, who was defining the "swing era"[10], was coming into increasing conflict with Mitch Miller at Columbia Records where he was signed. Novelty and gimmicks was the root of much of the success by the label's[11] artists and in 1952 they separated.

6. Now signed to Capitol Records[12], "The Voice" as he was sometimes known found his success beginning to slump. Rather than 8 a year he had only 1 Top Ten hit in a year and a half with 1953's *I'm Walking Behind You*. It appeared that now in his 30's, despite working with fine music arrangers like Nelson Riddle[13] and Gordon Jenkins[14], his potential to attract new teenage audiences had diminished. In 1954 however, the spotlight was upon him again when he won the Academy Award for Best Supporting Actor for his part in the World War II drama *From Here to Eternity*. Following this, 1955 saw the release of his ballad collection *In the Wee Small Hours*, which was later inducted into *the Grammy Hall of Fame*[15].

7. Throughout this period, Sinatra employed thematic concepts and alternated between albums devoted to slow arrangements (*In the Wee Small Hours*) and dance charts (*Swing Easy*). This in part allowed him to rule

**3** Did Sinatra's success seem to come too fast?

**4** Why does the author use the word "lend" in Line 1 of Paragraph 5?

**5** Using the certain period of time as the subject of one sentence is one of the author's favorite writing techniques, which appears in Paragraphs 5, 6 and 9. How does such sentence pattern impress you?

the LP charts while the rise of rock 'n' roll (Elvis and teen idols) ruled the singles.

8. In 1960, despite success and having not yet completed his recoding commitment to Capitol, Sinatra recorded the album *Ring-a-Ding-Ding* for his own label which he named Reprise Records. This led to 6 albums being released by the two labels in 1961 which all landed in the Top Ten. His popularity was only enhanced by the establishment of The Rat Pack (Dean Martin, Sammy Davis Jr., Peter Lawford, Joey Bishop, and Sinatra) which began to tour and perform together in movies and concerts. The Summit (as they called themselves) were instrumental in the rise of Las Vegas as a popular entertainment destination as they sold out constantly and would pop up on each other's bills. They helped too to desegregate the venues and hotels by refusing to play anywhere that enforced such separation. Sinatra's connections in Vegas and New Jersey however, attracted controversy as well due to circulating rumors of ties to the mafia. Such notions led to the revoking of his gaming license and a subpoena to testify in front of the New Jersey State Commission on organized crime. Such allegations were never substantiated yet many attribute the degree of his successes in the city of sin to such friends.

9. The end of the decade saw the Rat Pack split however, as a counterculture to the "establishment entertainment" arose. "The Chairman" (as he was known), continued with his solo success well into his 70's with notable releases like 1980's *Trilogy: Past, Present, Future* and 1993's *Duets* which sold more than 3 million copies (his most ever). Retiring in 1995 at the age of 80, he followed fellow Rat Pack members and close friends Martin and Davis and died 2 years later.

10. More than just his recordings, Sinatra left behind a legacy and a sound that many consider to define 20th century popular music. Followers like Tony Bennet, Tony Alamo, Bobby Darin and contemporary artists like Michael Buble and Harry Connick Jr. owe much of their success and that of their styles to *Old Blue Eyes*. His contribution is demonstrated not only by his sales but by his recognitions including 9 Grammy Awards (including 3 Albums of the Year), a Grammy Award for Lifetime Achievement, a Grammy Trustees Award (for

contributions outside of performance), a United States Congressional Gold Medal, an Academy Award, 3 Golden Globes and countless other honorary bestowments and nominations.

11. His record label too, which he built on the concept of creative freedom and artist's eventual ownership of their music and publishing, still exists today. Sold to Warner Bros. Records in 1963, Reprise functions now almost as a secondary parent company and boasts such artists as Neil Young, Eric Clapton and The Smashing Pumpkins[16].

6 After reading, are you convinced that Frank Sinatra is really SOMEBODY in popular music of the 20th century? Why?

## Notes

1. **in one's own right**   by reason of one's own ability or ownership etc.
2. **Sicilian** *a.*   of or relating to or characteristic of Sicily, Italy, or the people of Sicily
3. **trio** /ˈtrio/ *n.*   a musical composition for three performers
4. **Bing Crosby**   (May 3, 1903—Oct. 14, 1977) American singer and actor, one of the best-selling recording artists of the 20th century, with over half a billion records in circulation
5. **Billie Holiday**   (Apr. 7, 1915—Jul. 17, 1959) American jazz singer and songwriter. Nicknamed "Lady Day" by her friend and musical partner, Holiday had a seminal influence on jazz and pop singing. Her vocal style, strongly inspired by jazz instrumentalists, pioneered a new way of manipulating phrasing and tempo.
6. **Mabel Mercer**   (Feb. 3, 1900—Apr. 20, 1984) English-born cabaret singer who performed in the United States, Britain, and Europe with the greats in jazz and cabaret
7. **MGM**   Metro-Goldwyn-Mayer Pictures (commonly known as MGM) is an American media company, involved primarily in the production and distribution of films and television programs. Once simply the largest and most glamorous of the film studios, MGM was founded in 1924 when the entertainment entrepreneur Marcus Loew gained control of Metro Pictures, Goldwyn Pictures Corporation and Louis B. Mayer Pictures. Its headquarters is in Beverly Hills, California. On Nov. 3, 2010, MGM filed for bankruptcy.
8. **Gene Kelly**   (Aug. 23, 1912—Feb. 2, 1996) American dancer, actor, singer, film director and producer, and choreographer. Kelly was known for his energetic and athletic dancing style, his good looks and the likeable characters that he played on screen.
9. **vein** /ven/ *n.*   a distinctive style or manner
10. **the "swing era"**   (sometimes referred to as the "Big Band Era") the period of time (1935—1946) when big band swing music was the most popular music in the United States

11. label /'leibəl/ *n.*   trade name of a company that produces musical recordings
12. **Capitol Records**   a major American record label, formerly located in Los Angeles, but as of 2011[update] operating in New York City as part of Capitol Music Group. Its former headquarters building, the Capitol Tower, is a major landmark near the corner of Hollywood and Vine. It is a wholly owned subsidiary of EMI.
13. **Nelson Riddle**   (Jun. 1, 1921—Oct. 6, 1985) American arranger, composer, bandleader and orchestrator whose career stretched from the late 1940s to the mid 1980s
14. **Gordon Jenkins**   (May 12, 1910—May 1, 1984) American arranger, composer and pianist who was an influential figure in popular music in the 1940s and 1950s, renowned for his lush string arrangements
15. **the Grammy Hall of Fame**   established by The Recording Academy's National Trustees in 1973 to honor recordings of lasting qualitative or historical significance that are at least 25 years old
16. **the Smashing Pumpkins**   an American alternative rock band from Chicago, Illinois, formed in 1988

## A Critical Reader (II)

**1** If you are to briefly describe the legendary life of Frank Sinatra in no more than 100 words, what details will you cross out?

**2** As for those very important figures you have added to the list in "A Critical Reader (I)", did they walk through the same rugged road as Frank Sinatra did? Please offer some details to support your opinion.

## A Critical Writer

### I. Basic Writing Techniques

#### 1. Style and word choice

1.1   As a piece of biography, the article *Old Blue Eyes* is written for _____ (A. common B. highly educated   C. primary school   D. professional) readers. The purpose of the author is to _____ (A. narrate   B. persuade   C. describe   D. analyze) the extraordinary achievement in the entertainment circle made by the subject, Frank Sinatra.

Biography belongs to the category of _____ (A. Description   B. Argumentation   C. Narration   D. Exposition). In order not to be too subjective, the author seldom uses absolutes. Instead, some tentative expressions and sentence patterns are employed.

e.g.

(1) It appeared that now in his 30's, despite working with fine music arrangers like Nelson Riddle and Gordon Jenkins, his potential to attract new teenage audiences had diminished.

(2) This in part allowed him to rule the LP charts while the rise of rock n' roll (Elvis and teen idols) ruled the singles.

(3) Sold to Warner Bros. Records in 1963, Reprise functions now almost as a secondary parent company and boasts such artists as Neil Young, Eric Clapton and The Smashing Pumpkins.

Please put the following Chinese sentences, applying the given expressions for tentativeness.

1) 撰写本书时，普京依然是俄罗斯最得人心的政治家，也许是因为他在一定程度上恢复了俄罗斯人生活上的稳定和自尊。[probably]（《强人治国：普京传》）

_____
_____

2) 也许史蒂夫会说，他将生活中的点点滴滴都收集起来，这样他的灵感就能如充满活力的泉水般勃然喷发。[perhaps]（《我是乔布斯》）

_____
_____

3) 看起来，菲利普的这种想法比他构想天国的任何想法都更有吸引力。[appear]（《法兰西第一女杰：罗兰夫人传》）

_____
_____

4) 她拥有极高的名望和无数的成就，但是，她似乎并不快乐。[seem]（《惠特尼·休斯顿传》）

_____
_____

5) 这个说法似乎非常不可能，但却有可能与她成年后爱过的两个英国男人在头脑里有某种联系。[seemingly]（《可可·香奈儿的传奇一生》）

_____
_____

**1.2  Since this article is about a figure in popular music, the author employs many jargons. Jargon: The specialized or technical language of a trade, profession, or similar group.**

e.g.

(1) …, he got his first break in 1935 when his mother persuaded a local trio, The Three Flashes, to accept him and become The Hoboken Four.

(2) Appearing on the radio show *Major Bowes Amateur Hour* and winning a 6 month touring gig with the program, Sinatra was on his way.

(3) Rather than 8 a year he had only 1 Top Ten hit in a year and a half with 1953's *I'm Walking Behind You*.

Please read the article and pick out the rest jargons in the circle of pop music.

## 2. Basic rules for good sentences and paragraphs

### 2.1  Basic rules

1) Unity

Please read Paragraph 1 again and find out the central idea in this paragraph.

Arguably the most important figure in popular music of the 20th century, Frank Sinatra is unquestionably an American Icon for the ages. Singing and promoting the American song as it was written, Sinatra consistently took the "standards" of great composers and reinterpreted them in such a way as to establish them as classics in their own right. Despite countless changes in the times and popular tastes, he sustained a career spanning over 60 years and is revered still today.

2) Conciseness

Please paraphrase the following sentences, and see whether there are any words redundant.

(1) In the same year he recorded his first solo effort and Cole Porter's *Night and Day* become the first of what was to be countless chart entries under his own name.
_____
_____

(2) Now in his mid twenties he had become the first real teen idol revealing a whole new audience for pop music, the "bobby soxers".
_____
_____

(3) Novelty and gimmicks was the root of much of the success by the label's artists and in 1952 they separated.
_____
_____

(4) More than just his recordings, Sinatra left behind a legacy and a sound that many consider to define 20th century popular music.
_____
_____

3) Cohesion and Coherence

Please summarize the article and explain how these underlined judgments about Frank Sinatra in the first sentence "<u>Arguably the most important figure</u> in popular music of the 20th century, Frank Sinatra is <u>unquestionably an American Icon</u> for the ages." are clearly illustrated.

**Analysis:**

With three sentences only in the first paragraph, the central idea of this biography is clearly stated: Frank Sinatra has made extraordinary achievements in popular music of the 20th century. Starting from the second paragraph, the author narrates the key events which either contribute to or offset Sinatra's success. The subject's ups and downs naturally exemplify the judgment "arguably the most important figure". However, around 80% of the listed events are about Sinatra's approaching the summit of his success, which proves him to be the "unquestionably an American Icon".

### 3. Basic rule for good essays
#### 3.1 Questions
1) Are there enough details to support the central idea of this biography?
2) How are all events in this article organized?
#### 3.2 Analysis
Since biography is one type of narration, it must be made up of details. "There should be enough details so that the reader knows what is happening, but there should not be too many of them, or the reader will be confused and lose interest in the story. Only relevant details that contribute to bringing out the main idea of the narrative are useful and effective."[1]

In this article, all events employed by the author are pertinent to Sinatra's iconic achievements. Paragraph 2, which presents his starting-off on the way to success, introduces his birth place and year as well as his family and educational backgrounds in only one sentence. As about a biography, such introduction is indispensable. However, the author condenses many parts into one sentence without sacrificing anything necessary. Especially, the ending of that sentence makes readers understand why Sinatra could win his fame so young.

In the following paragraphs, Sinatra's steps upward to the summit of achievements are organized chronically, which is typical of a biography. As every other zigzagging road, Sinatra did not stride toward his final success smoothly. He confronted setbacks as well as astonishing successes. He deviated from his musical track to pictures and he played roles of a composer and a manager. Awards he won as well as profits he made, applauses for him as well as boos against him, combining to make him "the most important figure in popular music of the 20th century" arguably and "an American Icon for the ages" unquestionably.

#### 3.3 Working out an outline
Please work out an outline on the topic "A Look at the Life of…" with the subject being one figure in the circle of entertainment. Your outline is supposed to echo your purpose of choosing this figure as your writing subject.

## II. Specific Writing Techniques
How to write a short biography?

### 1. Definition of biography
Please complete the definition of "biography" with appropriate words.
A **biography** is _____ as a written history of a person's life. A biography paper

---
1 刘礼进主编:《实用英文写作》，中山大学出版社，2003，第82页。

can focus either on that person's entire _____, a specific section or _____, or just the highlights. What a biography should not be is a dry recitation of _____ that offers little insight into the importance or significance of the subject. A/An _____ biography also is one that recognizes the value of choosing the most influential aspects of the subject's life, making it _____ why a biography is being considered in the first place.

### 2. Significance of biography subject

Please find answers to the following questions in the text, <u>all of which induce to the purpose of writing the biography</u>.

1) What makes this person special or interesting?

2) What kind of effect did he or she have on the world/other people?

3) What are the adjectives you would most use to describe the person?

4) What examples from their life illustrate those qualities?

5) What events shaped or changed this person's life?

6) Did he or she overcome obstacles? Take risks? Get lucky?

7) Would the world be better or worse if this person hadn't lived? How and why?

### 3. Basic details in biography

Please find out the details listed below, <u>which should be included in a biography</u>.

• Date and place of birth and death

• Family information

• Lifetime accomplishments

• Major events of life

• Effects/impact on society, historical significance

### 4. Rules for writing an interesting short biography

#### 4.1 An interest-arousing beginning

Read the following beginning paragraphs or sentences of a few biographies. Find out the more interest-arousing ones and offer your reason.

1) "Late one afternoon in October, 1809, Meriwether Lewis arrived at a small log cabin nestled deep in the Tennessee Mountains. By sunrise on the following day, he was dead, having suffered gunshot wounds to the head and chest."

2) Counted among the 50 most beautiful people of 2000 by *People* magazine, Cruz's stunning looks have kept her busy in the movie business; being taken seriously is another day's work.

3) Hillary Rodham Clinton once said that "There cannot be true democracy unless women's voices are heard." In 2006, when Nancy Pelosi became the nation's first female Speaker of the House, one woman's voice rang out clear. With this development, democracy grew to its truest

level ever in terms of women's equality. The historical event also paved the way for Senator Clinton as she warmed her own vocal chords in preparation for a presidential race.

4) "As a young child, Charles Dickens was forced to work in a shoe polish factory. In *Hard Times*, Dickens taps into his childhood experience to explore the evils of social injustice and hypocrisy."

5) Allen, Woody (Allen Stewart Konigsberg), 1935— , American actor, writer, and director, one of contemporary America's leading filmmakers, b. Brooklyn, N.Y.

6) A sultry and sometimes playful Spanish actress, Penelope Cruz became famous internationally when she played the motion-sick heroine in the 2000 film Woman on Top. She was already a star in Spain

### 4.2 Interest-retaining recounting

1) **Chronological.** Go by the timeline, recounting each event in the order in which it happened. This is the simplest way to go, but it's difficult to support your thesis in this context.

2) **Flashbacks.** Describe a recent or current situation, then "flashback" to an earlier point in that person's life. This is good for illustrating cause and effect, or how this led to that. You can even go in complete reverse order; begin at the end, and work your way backwards.

3) **Work.** If the person's life is closely tied to his or her career, you can break it up by job positions or works created. This can be tied to phases or cycles in the subject's life.

4) **Accomplishments / Events.** One idea is to start and end with events that mirror each other in some way. Maybe you can start with a toy boat that the subject made when they were 5, and end off with a military submarine that they designed at age 55.

## III. Your Turn to Write an Essay

Please try to write biographies as the following instructions say.

1) Select a subject either living or dead but who was alive during your lifetime and of whom you have some memory. It is not necessary the person knows or knew you but only that you know of the person. Try to conduct one or two interviews with people who know or knew your subject either directly or from afar and if you can. Secure an interview with your subject. Rely on your own knowledge of the person and employ only a minimum of research other than interviews.

2) Repeat Exercise 1, but this time your subject must have died before you were born. You'll need to rely on more research, although depending on the circumstances, interviews might still be an option. Although you have no living recollection of your subject, you must get to know him/her and bring him/her to life for the reader.

## A Critical Reader (II)

1. Don't confuse fame with success. Madonna is one; Helen Keller is the other. —Erma Bombeck

2. In order to succeed, your desire for success should be greater than your fear of failure. —Bill Cosby

3. Success is getting what you want. Happiness is wanting what you get.

—Dale Carnegie

## Text B

### Warming up

1. Which sports star do you admire the most? Please list out at least three points to support your favor for him/her.
2. Would you agree that sports stars belong to the circle of entertainment? Why?

### The Jordan Mystique

By David L. Porter

**A Critical Reader (I)**

1. A monument stands in front of the United Center, home of the Chicago Bulls National Basketball Association[1] team. A 2,000-pound bronze statue features Michael Jordan in full flight, ready to slam dunk[2] the ball, to the chagrin[3] of cowering defenders. The front panel capsulizes the phenomenal athlete: "<u>The best there ever was. The best there ever will be.</u>"

① Can you find any proof to counter the underlined comments?

2. Jordan needs no introduction. He is among the best-known and wealthiest athletes in the history of organized sports. With the possible exceptions of <u>boxer Muhammad Ali</u> and <u>baseball player Babe Ruth</u>, no athlete has made a greater impact on American society. ESPN[4] in 1999 voted Jordan the greatest twentieth-century athlete, and the Associated Press[5] ranked him second, behind Babe Ruth[6]. Jordan has appeared on the cover of *Sports Illustrated* more than 50 times since 1983 and was named the magazine's "Sportsman of the Year" in 1991.

② Please make a brief introduction about the boxer Muhammad Ali and the baseball player Babe Ruth.

3. *Sports Illustrated* contributor Jack McCallum wrote that Jordan "stands alone on the mountaintop, unquestionably the most famous athlete on the planet and one of its most famous citizens of any kind." He called him a sportsman who "has surpassed every

standard by which we gauge the fame of an athlete and, with few exceptions, has handled the adulation with a preternatural grace and ease that have cut across the lines of race, age, and gender. He transcends sports."

4. After struggling initially, Jordan blossomed into a basketball star at Emsley A. Laney High School in Wilmington, North Carolina. He became a national celebrity as a freshman guard at the University of North Carolina, covering a 15-foot jump shot[7] in the waning seconds of the 1982 NCAA Championship game to defeat Georgetown University. Besides making All-America[8] as a sophomore and junior, Jordan was named *The Sporting News* Player of the Year in 1983 and 1984 and winner of the Naismith Award[9] and Wooden Award[10] in 1984. He co-captained the U.S. basketball team to a gold medal at the 1984 Summer Olympic Games in Los Angeles, California.

5. <u>Jordan's transcendence[11] stemmed partly from good timing</u>. Jordan joined the Chicago Bulls after his junior year in 1984, when the NBA was enjoying an era of unprecedented popularity. Americans were fascinated with the personal duels between two modern sports folk heroes, Larry Bird of the Boston Celtics and Magic Johnson of the Los Angeles Lakers. When Bird and Johnson retired in the early 1990s, Jordan almost single handedly propelled the NBA to even more stratospheric[12] levels of success and international visibility. Former coach Larry Brown observed, "I love Magic and Larry. But Michael ... I'd pay money to see him play. I'd pay money to see him practice."

6. Jordan led Chicago to six National Basketball Association titles in the 1990s. Between 1991 and 1993, the Bulls became the first team in three decades to win three consecutive NBA championships. He was selected NBA Most Valuable Player in 1988, 1991, and 1992 and became the only hoopster[13] ever voted NBA Finals MVP three straight times. He also starred for the U.S. Dream Team, gold medal winners in the 1992 Summer Olympic Games at Barcelona, Spain.

7. Jordan soared to even greater heights after a nearly two-year hiatus[14] to propel the Bulls to three more NBA titles from 1996 to 1998. Chicago shattered the NBA record for more victories in a single season with a 72—10 mark in 1995—1996, as Jordan became the first NBA player since

[3] How important do you feel "good timing" is to one's success, esp. to a sports star?

1970 to garner[15] MVP awards from the All-Star Game, regular season, and NBA Finals. The Bulls still dominated the NBA the next two seasons, with Jordan snagging NBA MVP honors in 1998 and NBA Finals MVP accolades[16] in 1997 and 1998. His intensive drive to win, extraordinary athletic ability, and uncanny basketball knowledge shown brilliantly when he battled influenza and personal fatigue to score the winning basket in Game 5 of the 1997 NBA Finals against the Utah Jazz.

8. Jordan retired from the Bulls in 1999, having led the NBA in scoring 10 times, including seven consecutive seasons, and won five NBA MVP awards. He is the only player to score at least 50 points in five playoff games and the only hoopster besides Wilt Chamberlain[17] to score more than 3,000 points in a season and average more than 30 points a game during his NBA career.

9. In January 2000, Jordan became president of basketball operations for the Washington Wizards and minority owner of the Washington Wizards Sports and Entertainment. He played for the Wizards from 2001 to 2003, helping rescue the franchise from a $20 million deficit to a $30 million profit in two years. Jordan did not lead the Wizards to the NBA playoffs, but he became just the fourth NBA player to score 30,000 career points and passed Chamberlain as the third leading scorer in NBA history. In June 2006, he became the second largest shareholder of the Charlotte Bobcats, fulfilling his dream of sharing in the ownership of an NBA club in North Carolina.

10. Jordan's transcendence stemmed from his phenomenal athleticism and personal magnetism. Coach Bob Knight in 1995 proclaimed, "Michael Jordan is the best that will ever play this game." Even those who never saw Jordan play a college or professional basketball recognize him. He combined exceptional athletic ability with a relatively clean public image. *Gentleman's Quarterly* correspondent David Breskin termed him "the most admired, idolized, and moneyed team-sport hero in the entire American-hero business. For some folks he has come to represent America." Sociologist Harry Edwards declared, "if I were charged with introducing an alien life form to the epitome of human potential, creativity, perseverance, and spirit, I would introduce that alien life form to Michael Jordan."

4 How much do you know about the "American-hero business" underlined in Paragraph 10?

## Notes

1. **the National Basketball Association** (NBA) the pre-eminent men's professional basketball league in North America. It consists of thirty franchised member clubs, of which twenty-nine are located in the United States and one in Canada. It is an active member of USA Basketball (USAB), which is recognized by the International Basketball Federation as the national governing body for basketball in the United States. The NBA is one of the 4 major North American professional sports leagues. NBA players are the world's best paid sportsmen, by average annual salary per player.
2. **dunk** /dʌŋk/ *n.* a basketball shot in which the basketball is propelled downward into the basket; *v.* make a dunk shot, in basketball
3. **chagrin** /ʃəˈgrin/ *n.* strong feelings of embarrassment
4. **ESPN** American global cable television network focusing on sports-related programming including live and pre-taped event telecasts, sports talk shows, and other original programming. Its name derives from "Entertainment and Sports Programming Network".
5. **the Associated Press:** an American news agency. The AP is a cooperative owned by its contributing newspapers, radio and television stations in the United States, which both contribute stories to the AP and use material written by its staff journalists. Many newspapers and broadcasters outside the United States are AP subscribers, paying a fee to use AP material without being contributing members of the cooperative.
6. **Babe Ruth** (Feb. 6, 1895—Aug. 16, 1948) nicknamed "the Bambino", American baseball player who spent 22 seasons in Major League Baseball (MLB) playing for three teams (1914—1935), and one of the first five players to be elected into the National Baseball Hall of Fame
7. **jump shot** /dʒʌmp ʃɔt/ *n.* a player releases the basketball at the high point of a jump
8. **All-America** An All-America team is an honorary sports team composed of outstanding amateur players—those considered the best players of a specific season for each team position—who in turn are given the honorific "All-America" and typically referred to as "All-American athletes", or simply "All-Americans".
9. **Naismith Award** a basketball award named after Dr. James Naismith, and awarded by the Atlanta Tipoff Club. The Naismith Award can be:
    - Naismith College Player of the Year (men's and women's; NCAA Division I basketball)
    - Naismith College Coach of the Year (men's and women's; NCAA Division I basketball)
    - Naismith Prep Player of the Year (male and female)
    - Naismith Outstanding Contribution to Basketball (male or female; overall impact on basketball)
    - Naismith College Official of the Year (men's and women's)

> 10. **Wooden Award** an award given annually to the most outstanding men's and women's college basketball players. The program consists of the men's and women's Player of the Year awards, the Legends of Coaching award and recognizes the All—America Teams.
> 11. **transcendence** /træn'sendəns/ *n.* the state of excelling or surpassing or going beyond usual limits
> 12. **stratospheric** /ˌstætəusˈferik/ *a.* adjective form of the noun stratosphere, which means "any great height or degree, as the highest point of a graded scale"
> 13. **hoopster** /ˈhuːpstə/ *n.* basketball player, with the noun "hoop" referring to "horizontal circular band with a net through which players try to throw the basketball"
> 14. **hiatus** /haiˈeitəs/ *n.* a natural opening or perforation through a bone or a membranous structure
> 15. **garner** /ˈɡɑːnə/ *v.* acquire or deserve by one's efforts or actions
> 16. **accolade** /ˈækəˌleid/ *n.* a tangible symbol signifying approval or distinction; "an award for bravery"
> 17. **Wilt Chamberlain** (Aug. 21, 1936—Oct. 12, 1999) American basketball player, widely considered one of the greatest and most dominant players in NBA history

## A Critical Reader (II)

**1** Compared with Text A, what are the differences you can find, both in the biography subjects and in the writing styles?

**2** Please find out three words you feel most suitable to describe Michael Jordan's dazzling career.

## A Critical Writer

### I. Style and Structure

As Text A, this article is another _____ which has been _____ structured.

Please list out the events about Michael Jordan mentioned in this biography in the following chart in the time line.

| Year | Name of the Team | Place | Role in the Team | Event | Awards |
|---|---|---|---|---|---|
|  | Emsley A. Laney High School Team | Wilmington, North Carolina |  | blossomed into a basketball star |  |
| 1982 |  |  |  |  |  |
| 1983 |  |  |  |  |  |
| 1984 |  |  |  |  |  |
| 1988 |  |  |  |  |  |
| 1991 |  |  |  |  |  |
| 1992 |  |  |  |  |  |
| 1993 |  |  |  |  |  |
| 1995 |  |  |  |  |  |
| 1996 |  |  |  |  |  |
| 1997 |  |  |  |  |  |
| 1998 |  |  |  |  |  |
| 1999 |  |  |  |  |  |
| 2000 |  |  |  |  |  |
| 2001 |  |  |  |  |  |
| 2003 |  |  |  |  |  |
| 2006 |  |  |  |  |  |

## II. Word Choices

It's obvious that David L. Porter, author of this biography, spares no efforts to glorify Michael Jordan's unprecedented achievements.

Please find out all complimentary expressions the author uses to describe Michael Jordan, and categorize them in the following chart according to their parts of speech.

| Adjective | Noun | Verb |
|---|---|---|
| phenomenal | star | transcend |
|  |  |  |
|  |  |  |
|  |  |  |
|  |  |  |
|  |  |  |
|  |  |  |
|  |  |  |

## III. Your Turn to Write

### 1. Outlining

Please choose one sports star, collect as much information about him/her as you can, and list them out as you have done in "1. Style and Structure". If possible, divide the events into a few stages.

### 2. Writing

Please write a short biography of no more than 1,000 words, based on the above outline you have drawn. Don't forget to employ enough words of different parts of speech to demonstrate your attitude toward this sports star.

## Pearls of Wisdom

1. Basketball is like war in that offensive weapons are developed first, and it always takes a while for the defense to catch up. —Red Auerbach

2. Good, better, best. Never let it rest. Until your good is better and your better is best. —Tim Duncan

3. If winning isn't everything, why do they keep score? — Vince Lombardi

## Text C

### Warming up

1. How much do you know about Elvis Presley?
2. Do you like the Chinese version "猫王" of Elvis Presley's nickname *Hillbilly Cat*? Why or why not?

## Dressing as the Hillbilly Cat

By Susan Doll, PhD

### A Critical Reader

1. When looking at photos of Elvis with the Blue Moon Boys, you immediately notice that the Hillbilly Cat stands out. Moore and Black often wore their western-style Starlite Wranglers costumes or white shirts with ties. Elvis, on the other hand, preferred the style of clothing that black rhythm-and-blues artists often wore.

[1] What's the original meaning of the word "hillbilly"? What kind of effect does this title have on Elvis Presley's fame?

Flashy, hip, bold, and urban, this type of clothing could be purchased on Beale Street, where the black night clubs and hot spots were located. Among the most respected shops on Beale Street was Lansky Brothers, which was operated by Guy and Bernard Lansky.

2. Elvis favored pleated pants with wide legs. These pants virtually vibrated when Elvis bounced on the balls of his feet while performing. He seemed to like trousers with stripes down the sides, because years later several people recalled seeing him in <u>pink</u>-striped and <u>white</u>-striped pants. Big baggy suit coats in <u>white</u> or <u>black</u> draped his thin body, while <u>brightly colored</u> ties in gaudy patterns rounded out the ensemble. However, sometimes he preferred tight, high-collared shirts in <u>bright</u> colors with the sleeves rolled up. <u>Pink</u> and <u>black</u> were his favorite colors, so, of course, he wore a <u>pink</u> and <u>black</u> suit for his first appearance on the *Louisiana Hayride*. But, he also was fond of his sea green bolero jacket, which he wore with a mariner's cap.

3. Elvis' wardrobe was certainly atypical of the western-style costumes associated with both male and female country artists at the time, which featured kerchiefs around the neck, Stetson hats, and shirts embroidered with patterns and trimmed with piping. However, some of these western costumes, such as those worn by Porter Wagoner and Hank Thompson, were actually quite gaudy with colored rhinestones and brightly colored patterns sewn onto the fronts, sleeves, and backs. So Elvis' Beale Street clothing wasn't any gaudier than that of typical country artists. Instead, he stood out because he dressed like African American R&B artists. Elvis dressed in his Beale Street attire both on stage and off, but he was fond of capping his look onstage with eye makeup and a carefully sculpted ducktail haircut.

4. Elvis' ducktail hairstyle took a long time to perfect and required three different hair products. He used a thick pomade to slick back the hair high on his head (though one carefully chosen strand always fell over his eyes while he performed). Another product slicked back the sides, and a third was used to form the central part that ran form the crown of the head to the nape of his neck. The effect resembled the rear end of a duck, so a less-polite name for this hairstyle developed: the duckass, or d.a.

**2** Will you make a psychological analysis on Elvis's preference for bright colors, esp. pink and white, while favoring the contradictory black?

**3** How much can this spectacular hairstyle contribute to Elvis' success?

## A Critical Reader (II)

1. Please collect some more details about Elvis Presley's influence on American culture.
2. Please briefly describe another pop music star that influences fashion in the 21st century.

## A Critical Writer

### I. Style

Narration often goes hand in hand with _____[1].

When _____ a person, the author may first give details of his/her appearance. Then he should try to reveal the person's character, thoughts, and feelings, which may be shown in what the person does and says, in how he behaves to others. And it is important to grasp his characteristic features which distinguish him from all other people.[1]

Please summarize the characters of Elvis Presley based on the vivid description in this excerpt of biography and quote the details to support your idea.

### II. Word Choices

Since this excerpt of biography illustrates Elvis Presley as an idol of fashion, many terms related fashion and clothes are employed.

Please gather all fashion terms and try to classify them into different categories, based on their different functions, like hairstyle, material, etc.

### III. Your Turn to Write

Please describe in detail the pop music star you have mentioned in "A Critical Reader(II)" so as to present your readers with an image of fashion icon.

## Pearls of Wisdom

1. From the time I was a kid, I always knew something was going to happen to me. Didn't know exactly what. —Elvis Presley

2. I'm not trying to be sexy. It's just my way of expressing myself when I move around. —Elvis Presley

3. It's human nature to gripe, but I'm going ahead and doing the best I can.
—Elvis Presley

---

1 刘礼进主编：《实用英文写作》，中山大学出版社，2003，第79页。

# Corpus-based Exercises (8)

## I. Key Word: fame

1. *Fame* is the thematic term in these three biographies. Please study the following chart taken from a corpus of college English texts, and categorize the collocations of *fame* based on different structures.

| | | |
|---|---|---|
| missionary outreach . / As her | fame | grew , so did her honors . Among |
| stein was not motivated by a desire for | fame | , said Simonton . Instead , his obs |
| been made of the potential for great | fame | to ruin football 's most gifted play |
| West has given Yao more wealth and | fame | than he ever could have imagined |
| experiments . / Antinori shot to | fame | seven years ago helping grandma   5 |
| ic / Grant Wood instantly rose to | fame | in 1930 with his painting Americ |
| rtrait . / Nan later remarked that the | fame | she gained from American Gothic |
| in rags who gave his creator permanent | fame | . / Other countries—France , |
| ubtful if he would have achieved world | fame | . And the English would have bee |
| the ranks of Hollywood stars . His huge | fame | gave him the freedom—and , mo   10 |
| Sussel left his native country to find | fame | and fortune on the streets of New |
| accepted . " He was bewildered by his | fame | : people wanted to meet him ; stra |
| l listen . But a hero goes beyond mere | fame | . / Heroes serve powers or pri |
| every standard by which we gauge the | fame | of an athete and , with few except |

Fame + V. _____
N. + Prep. + fame _____
A. + fame _____
N. and fame _____
V. (+ Prep.) + fame _____

2. Please employ the collocations listed above in appropriate forms to translate the Chinese sentences below.

1) 出名要趁早，来得太晚的话，快乐也不那么痛快。(《张爱玲传：独爱临水照花人》)

_____

2) 这些嬉皮士中有一个声名远扬的高手，他就是约翰·德拉浦。(《活着就为改变世界——乔布斯传》)

_____

3) 法国大革命产生了很多著名的人物，其中，鲜有人比罗兰夫人名声更大、更值得注意。（《法兰西第一女杰：罗兰夫人传》）

4) 对于很多年轻人来说，他们对Facebook的创始人马克·扎克伯格其实早就有所耳闻，因为他有着不菲的身价。（《现在，我们接管世界（马克·扎克伯格传）》）

## II. Key Word: rank

*Rank* is a term frequently employed in Text B. In fact, in the circle of both entertainment, "rank", as a noun, means almost everything. Please categorize the collocations of "rank" according its parts of speech, and put them into appropriate Chinese expressions.

| | | |
|---|---|---|
| d reality . ) / Contrasting value : | **Rank** | and status : People 's roles are defined in ter |
| the Buddha and was granted a high | rank | Heaven . Monkey was made God of Victori |
| rst place , the hat served as a sign of | rank | throughout most of history , a visible m |
| show " face " to someone of higher | rank | . Richard Tallboy , CEO of the World Coal |
| e but too flashy for someone of his | rank | at the company . / His wife drives him to     5 |
| n . / Salaryman has risen to the | rank | of section manager . His job consists largely |
| futures . Few people ever reach the | rank | of department manager and Salaryman is be |
| ? Conversational ability ? Asked to | rank | such attributes , most intellectuals put physi |
| d foremost as an ardent desire for | rank | , fame , or power " . Isn't that too narrow ? S |
| he American alternative to social | rank | based on family background . Business is    10 |
| n easy way to establish the social | rank | order . When your dog obeys a simple requ |
| othing , while whites of the same | rank | received $1 3 per month plus clothing . Onl |
| he asked 12 5 undergraduates to | rank | two groups of photographs , one of men and |
| tical offices . They were asked to | rank | them again , in the order they would vote for |
| er into the dank lower decks , the | rank | smell of salt and rotting seaweed , the fetid   15 |
| ads of white cotton which are his | rank | , his whole adult life . Thirty years . Gulls sh |
| at obtaining some advantage in | rank | or fortune , nobody wishes them success . N |

1. **rank** *n.*

2. **rank** *v.*

# Future Plans

> **Warming up**
>
> Four years in college could be a long time. However, it is never too early to make a plan for your life after graduation.
> 1. What was your dream at the very beginning of college life? Do you still hold that dream, or have you changed your mind?
> 2. What is your plan for the near future? Are you going to take a job immediately after graduation, or to pursue a higher academic degree, or are you ambitious enough to begin your own business?

## Text A

### Life after Graduation: To Work or Not to Work?

GoPinoy.com

1. All college or university graduates often face this type of dilemma: What's next after graduation? Should I start working after graduation? Would it be smarter to consider pursuing a postgraduate study? Should I put up a business instead? Or take a break before thinking about joining the workforce? Questions like these would always pop up[1].

2. But before even thinking of what to do next, the best way to avoid these dilemmas is to prepare before you graduate; get your plans organized and get the right advice from the right people. Getting advice is very important since it's going to be your first time out on the "real world". Experienced and well-informed people are needed to help you weigh out your best options even if you have decided on what to do next. Universities and colleges offer career services where help is obtainable.

3. If you finally opt to[2] work after graduation after careful thought, then start finding details on job

### A Critical Reader (I)

[1] The author has listed several categories of plans after graduation. Which one do you fall in?

[2] Does your college have career services offered? Have you ever seek help from experienced people about job hunting?

[3] What is the structural function of Paragraph 2?

placements and job vacancies³. Your college or university career service can assist you with your applications, interview techniques and CVs⁴. Even former graduates can avail of⁵ these services. You can as well search for jobs online, in trade journals or in newspapers. If you are curious on what it would be like to work on a specific career, you can always discover them while you're still at the university. Better yet, try volunteering where you can enhance your skills and to give you an early work experience. A previous working experience is one quality that an employer mostly looks into from a resume.

**4** Have you ever worked as an interne? What was your job like? Was the pay satisfactory?

4. Some might prefer to pursue a postgraduate study after graduating. Before you even consider this, it's essential to think about your options, ideally, at least 18 months before you actually start a postgraduate course. Postgraduate studies are for you if:

**5** So far, have you got any idea about the postgraduate study in your major?

• You are interested of studying a more in-depth subject or want that first step to become a part of the academic field.

• You want to qualify for a specific career, helping you to stand out among other job applicants.

5. But you should also bear in mind that having more degrees doesn't guarantee more money in return. Do not settle for making education as a reason for you to avoid the strenuous⁶ task of job hunting. Do not go back to school unless you are certainly sure that you will be able to use what you'll learn to get ahead in the future. Be confident that the investment for studying further will pay off and not just let you end up taking a job that you could have gotten even without the additional degree.

**6** Why does higher degree not bring in more money?

6. For those who prefer to start their own business after graduation, feel free to consult your university if they're offering support to students and graduates wanting to start a business. They might provide you an option to increase your entrepreneurial⁷ skills as part of your course, or giving extra-curricular counsel sessions on starting a business. Some colleges also provide a starting service to guide graduates to get their business to soar. You can always ask your instructor for details.

**7** How much do you know about policies concerning college students starting their own business?

7. Lastly, if graduating students still opt to choose taking a break after graduation, then think of what you may be missing out. As the saying goes, "those who delay to play often pay"; potential employers could contact you the soonest if you'll be able to make your presence

**8** Why should one settle down his plan before taking a break?

known earlier to them after you graduate. It may even take weeks or months to get that first job out after college; so the earlier you start, the better.

8. Although you might feel that rewarding yourself after the hard work of spending years in school is something you deserve. This is reasonable enough, but you should at least organize your career plans before you go off on a break; it might be more difficult to embark[8] on a job search when you choose to set it aside first. You can enjoy taking the time off better once your game plan is already organized. Finally, whenever you feel the need to start looking for a job, make sure you integrate in[9] everything that you've discovered about yourself while having your post-college quest[10]; think of how you can use that knowledge in your future career.

9. Whatever your choice is, make sure you're happy and satisfied with it. Any path you choose to take that leads you to become a better person is definitely a path worth journeying on.

[9] What is the structural function of Paragraph 9?

### Notes

1. pop up *v.*   appear in a place or situation unexpectedly
2. opt to *v.*   choose or decide to do something in preference to anything else
3. vacancy /ˈveikənsi/ *n.*   a job or position which has not been filled
4. CV *n.*   short for curriculum vitae, a brief written account of your personal details, your education and jobs you have had
5. avail of *v.*   accept the offer and make use of it
6. strenuous /ˈstrɛnjuəs/ *a.*   involving a lot of effort or energy
7. entrepreneurial /ˌɔntrəprəˈnəːriəl/ *a.*   of or about company
8. embark /ɛmˈbɑrk/ *v.*   start doing something new, difficult or exciting
9. integrate in *v.*   combine
10. quest /kwɛst/ *n.*   a long and difficult search for something

## A Critical Reader (II)

[1] In this essay, the author proposes quite a few pieces of advice for each alternative plan after graduation. Do you agree with him? Is there any advice that you think is irrational? Why?

2️⃣ Among taking a job, continuing to study, and starting your own business, which one fit you most? Why? Or can you come up with a fourth choice besides them, if none of them suits your situation?

## A Critical Writer

### I. Basic Writing Techniques

#### 1. Basic rules for good sentences and paragraphs

As we have repeated in every chapter, a good paragraph should exhibit at least three traits: **coherence/cohesion, conciseness** and **unity**. Can you analyze how this essay has achieved these effects?

1.1 Read Paragraph 3 again and examine how cohesion/coherence is realized.

If you finally opt to work after graduation after careful thought, then start finding details on job placements and job vacancies. Your college or university career service can assist you with your applications, interview techniques and CVs. Even former graduates can avail of these services. You can as well search for jobs online, in trade journals or in newspapers. If you are curious on what it would be like to work on a specific career, you can always discover them while you're still at the university. Better yet, try volunteering where you can enhance your skills and to give you an early work experience. A previous working experience is one quality that an employer mostly looks into from a resume.

1.2 Analysis

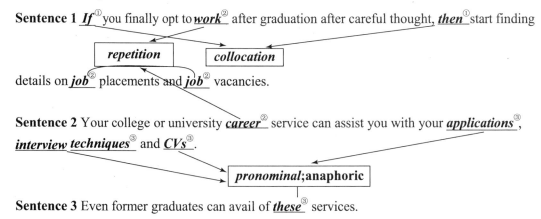

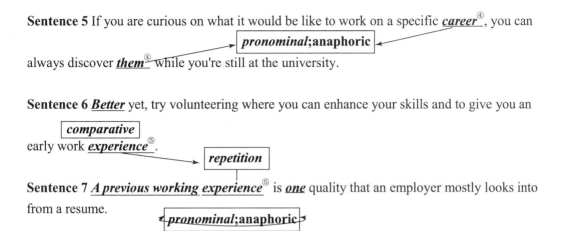

**Sentence 5** If you are curious on what it would be like to work on a specific *career*[4], you can always discover *them*[4] while you're still at the university.

**Sentence 6** *Better* yet, try volunteering where you can enhance your skills and to give you an early work *experience*[5].

**Sentence 7** *A previous working experience*[5] is *one* quality that an employer mostly looks into from a resume.

### 1.3 Exercises

From the analysis in 1.2, we can see that a good paragraph owns a clear and tight cohesion and coherence between and inside the sentences, with which the paragraph is organized logically and naturally. Examine the following paragraph. Can you see any cohesive/coherent relations in it? Put it in the right order according to cohesion and coherence, and cross redundant words, if there are any.

[1] Kaya also holds the degree of Special Distinction, as a member of the National Forensic League. [2] She has won many awards on the speech and debate circuits, and she has qualified for national tournaments. [3] The academics at Eastern Little Hope are most challenging, and Kaya fulfilled all the requirements with the added challenge of honors and advanced courses. [4] Success in these interscholastic activities requires extensive research and persuasive skills. [5] Kaya is an outstanding extemporaneous speaker and debater.

_____
_____
_____
_____
_____

### 1.4 Read Paragraph 3 again and do the following exercises.

[1] If you finally opt to work after graduation after careful thought, then start finding details on job placements and job vacancies. [2] Your college or university career service can assist you with your applications, interview techniques and CVs. [3] Even former graduates can avail of these services. [4] You can as well search for jobs online, in trade journals or in newspapers. [5] If you are curious on what it would be like to work on a specific career, you can always discover them while you're still at the university. [6] Better yet, try volunteering where you can enhance your skills and to give you an early work experience. [7] A previous working experience is one quality that an employer mostly looks into from a resume.

**Now based on the review, answer the questions below.**

1) What is the central theme of the paragraph? Which sentence serves as the topic sentence?

2) How do the rest sentences relate to and support the topic sentence?

3) Can you figure out the logical structure of the paragraph?

**1.5　Analysis:**

In **Paragraph 3**, we can easily see how unity is achieved.

The topic sentence in this paragraph is **Sentence (1)**, expressing the central theme that one should make some preparation if he decides to work after graduation.

**Sentence 2—7** are the supporting part to the topic sentence, talking about various sources from which one can get helped in finding a job.

In **Sentence 2**, the author points out career service in college or university can help one with applications, Interview technique and CVs.

In **Sentence 3**, the author suggests one go to former graduates for advice.

In **Sentence 4**, the author tells us internet, journals and newspapers are also helpful for job information.

In **Sentence 5**, the author suggests one do some research about a specific job if one is interested in it.

In **Sentence 6—7**, the author comes up with another way to figure out the details about a job—offering volunteer work in a company in this specific field, which is also quite useful when one is in the real hunting process.

**1.6　Exercise: Imitation**

Please translate the following Chinese into English, imitating the writing techniques in Paragraph 3.

1) 去目标公司面试之前，我们需要作一些准备工作。了解公司近年来的运营情况，以及在这种情况下公司对所求岗位潜在的特殊需求；再次自我评估，不断发掘自身贴合岗位需求的特质，并尽量缩小自身其他条件与岗位需求之间的差距。

_____

_____

_____

_____

2) 选择研究生阶段的专业方向并不是一件很容易的事情。我们需要明确自身的研究兴趣，并且在研究兴趣与研究能力之间选择一个平衡点。同时，该专业毕业生的就业率及就业去向也是另一大不得不考虑的因素。

_____

_____

_____

_____

3) 大学生自主创业是现今十分时髦的现象。与求职、考研的准备工作相比，筹划自主创业更是一项庞大的工程。一方面……另一方面……另外……（请根据主题句补全省略处）

_____
_____
_____
_____

## 2. Basic rule for good essays: Well-organized structure

In terms of structure, Text A is well-organized with introduction, body and conclusion clearly knitted and working together to complete the author's suggestion.

### 2.1 Questions

1) Which sentence is the thesis statement of the essay?
2) How does the author support his thesis statement?
3) In what way is the essay ended? Does it leave you a deep impression?

### 2.2 Analysis

**Paragraph 1—2** serve as the introduction part of the essay. **Paragraph (1)** is the lead-in, telling people what the essay is going to discuss: different choices faced by college graduates. **Paragraph 2** makes clear the author's opinion (thesis statement): *prepare before you graduate; get your plans organized and get the right advice from the right people.*

**Paragraph 3—8** is the supporting parts of the thesis statement, giving specific advice to graduates with different choices.

In **Paragraph 3**, the author gives advice to graduate who decide to take a job after graduation: *start finding details on job placements and job vacancies.*

In **Paragraph 4—5**, the author suggests graduates who want pursue higher academic degree think about it carefully and warns them that higher degree does not mean more money.

In **Paragraph 6**, the author encourages graduates who prefer to start their own business to consult the college/university.

In **Paragraph 7—8**, the author discourages graduates to take a break before making any preparation for future career.

**Paragraph 9** is the conclusion part, where the author ensures graduates to choose whichever path to become better.

### 2.3 Working out an outline

Based on the analysis above, work out an outline on the topic of "Preparation before meeting the recruiter", and make sure its structure is clear and logical. You may resort to the "Writing Process" in the Introduction of this book. Your writing plan should address at least the following questions:

1) How many parts and paragraphs do you plan to write?

2) What is the main idea for each paragraph?
3) What kind of details will you use to illustrate your point?

**2.4  Exercise: Rewriting**

In this essay, the author gives advice for college/university graduates about how to make preparation in accordance with their choice. In Paragraph 3, the author talks about what to do if one decides to work after graduation. Rewrite Paragraph 3, giving suggestions to graduates who want to continue to get a higher academic degree but are not very clear how to choose the major.

If you finally opt to _____ after careful thought, then _____. Your college or university _____ can assist you with _____. Even former graduates can avail of _____. You can as well search for _____ online, in _____ or in _____. If you are curious on what it would be like to _____, you can always discover them while you're still _____. Better yet, _____ and _____. A previous _____ is one quality that _____.

## II. Your Turn to Write

Nowadays, it is no easy to find a job for graduates. Besides professional skills and expertise, one also has to spend much effort in preparing for the recruiting link. Have you ever faced the recruiters? Or have you heard other people's legendary recruiting stories? What do you think one should pay special attention to before going over to the recruiter? Write an essay about the issue and give suggestions.

### Pearls of Wisdom

1. A graduation ceremony is an event where the commencement speaker tells thousands of students dressed in identical caps and gowns that 'individuality' is the key to success. —Robert Orben

2. Wherever you go, no matter what the weather, always bring your own sunshine. —Anthony J. D'Angelo

3. There is a good reason they call these ceremonies "commencement exercises." Graduation is not the end; it's the beginning. —Orrin Hatch

# Text B

> **Warming up**
>
> 1 Have you designed a practical future plan, for yourself, for the next five years?
> 2 Would you list the top three key factors contributive to one's success? Support your "billboard" with reasons.

## Priority Setting—Why?

By Laverne Forest & Sheila Mulcahy

**A Critical Reader (I)**

1. There are many reasons to set priorities. Some are important to the clientele[1] groups and larger society we serve; some are important for us to do our jobs well. These reasons fall into five categories:

**I. Priority setting is important to meet the changing needs and roles of our audiences.**

2. <u>The world is changing at a faster pace than ever before. People change, their roles in life change, their needs and problems change.</u> Problems are becoming more complex and interrelated as time goes by. People are better educated and demand more of us today than they did in the past—both in quality and quantity. New laws and regulations on the environment, population distribution, pesticides, etc., demand educational as well as legal input. The interrelatedness of problems and institutions creates more challenges for Extension professionals than in the past. No longer are our programs strictly rural oriented. The farm population has changed and shifted. Much of it has moved to the cities and towns. Farms are getting bigger and more specialized. The need for better farm production on less land is greater now than ever before, and the farmer's needs are more complex. People in big cities and small towns need help with their specific problems—and the problems are growing daily.

3. If Extension is a problem-solving institution, and if Extension agents are indeed change agents, we must help people respond not only to present needs and crises,

■ Have you realized the importance of setting priorities before reading this article?

■ Please take yourself, a university student, as an example and describe the change of your roles, needs and problems in the past five years.

but also to problems of the future: How to deal with new technologies? <u>What constitutes a healthy human being?</u> How can we help people prepare for the changes the future will demand?

4. But Extension resources are limited. We can't be all things to all people, even though the demands are great. Setting priorities and sticking to them is the only way to apply glue to a problem instead of a watery paste that spreads itself thin over many projects—and wears off in a short time.

5. Extension priorities and our program priorities must not merely follow the trends of society. We must be in the advance guard of future problems, to prevent them before they occur or to help people meet them when they're inevitable. We must be flexible enough to respond to people's needs, but firm enough to stick with priorities and reach defined goals.

**II. Priority setting helps us prevent future crisis.**

6. President Kennedy once said he asked experts to advise him "not what should I do, but what will happen if I do?"

7. We must take the consequences of our actions into account as we set priorities so we can make judgments about what we do in the present. What will happen if I do or don't do something?

8. Doing something, for instance, may be the cause of a future crisis. What we envision as a cure may end up being worse than the disease. Phosphates[2] brought us whiter wash loads, but with them came lake pollution. The dangers of DDT[3] may be worse than the bugs it was supposed to destroy.

9. On the other hand, a crisis may occur if we don't do something. If a riverside community doesn't build a dike or institute flood plain zoning, massive property and crop damage will surely result in a flood year. Or what will happen to productive farmlands if zoning[4] and restrictions aren't instituted near urban areas?

10. <u>Seeing the effect of past actions on our present lives will help us look ahead to see the effect of our present actions on the future.</u> Trying to see the future consequences of our present actions is an important part of setting priorities so that we can either prevent a crisis or avoid causing one. It will help us weigh risks and reduce

[3] What do you believe constitutes a healthy human being?

[4] Can you find an eight-character Chinese expression to translate the underlined sentence in Paragraph 10?

uncertainty about the probability of future consequences occurring and thus make more rational decisions. We must also look ahead to the future needs of people and plan action now to meet those needs. For instance, if we know that advanced technology and increased population will bring more unemployment, what can we do about it now? We also need to plan time for emerging, "time-is-right" concerns. For instance, a fuel shortage causes people to be more urgently concerned about energy conservation or seeking new sources of energy. Can we plan our time to allow for educational efforts in conjunction with people's concern over the future?

**III. Priority setting helps our credibility and accountability.**

11. We set priorities to get concrete results on important problems. These results will be noticed by those who demand we be accountable for our programs: Extension administration, legislatures, the county board, our clientele, and our community.

12. More and more, people external to Extension are holding us accountable for program results they see as important. They ask: What are you doing? What do you have to show for the resources we've invested? What difference have you made in the lives of people you work with and for? Are your activities worth the tax dollars or grants provided to support them? Our credibility increases when we show results and measure up to what we've said our priorities are. If others help us set priorities and are aware of them, they can see how we meet those priorities. They'll see how we apply our resources to problems and "put our money where our mouth is." Successful activities build credibility, trust, and cooperation. Our credibility will be high only if we actually carry out actions other people can see, to meet goals they recognize as important.

**IV. Priority setting helps make our Extension jobs easier**

13. If we commit ourselves, and use our commitments to guide our activities, it will be easier for us to know what to do and when to do it. First, we must commit ourselves to setting some priorities and then to carrying out a few selected priority programs. Having a priority set and seeing it as critically important helps us make

time to carry it out. If a choice is congruent with our own values and what we determine is important, commitment to the priority decision will come easily.

14. Setting priorities helps the person burdened with too many tasks break those tasks down by importance and get the most important things done first. It helps those locked into traditional activities, by habit or demand, become more open to new and changing priority problems. We can plan our programs more realistically and develop plans of work that tell what actually needs to be done to reach priority goals, and what actions we've designed to meet those goals. Our jobs become easier if others are aware of our priorities and adjust their expectations accordingly. We must discover the priorities of others, use them to decide ours, and communicate ours to them if we expect their involvement and help.

**V. Priority setting helps us allocate resources, coordinate our programs with others, and provide balanced programming.**

15. Setting priorities on the most critical needs and problems, and then setting priorities on our activities, allows us more efficient use of our limited resources. If we set priorities, back-up help, money, time, and cooperation with other agencies or the organization will be better coordinated and more likely to be available when we need them. Knowing the priorities of Extension and other personnel, and letting them know our priorities will help coordinate country, area, and statewide programs to deal with problems of most urgency. We're not setting priorities by ourselves.

16. For instance, in light of predicted food shortages and high prices, an agricultural agent can plan programs to improve livestock production; a community development agent can concentrate on land use planning to save precious farm acreage; a home agent might program on low-cost nutrition; and a horticulture specialist could help people use home gardens as a supplement to store-bought food. All can work together on education for actions to relieve one acute community problem with dire future consequences. Such coordination in planning priority programs for an entire community, or even for an entire state, will help reach all segments of the population who need help, despite a

limited amount of time, staff, and other resources. One agent or specialist can't do this alone.

**Summary**

17. <u>Setting priorities as individuals and as an organization helps us aim our limited resources at the most critical problems. By so doing, we'll increase our impact, be more efficient and more credible, reach more people, help prevent crises, enjoy our work more, minimize risk and uncertainty, plan more realistically, keep our work up to date with changing needs, and use our resources more wisely</u>. These are reasons why we need to set priorities.

from *First Things First—a Handbook of Priority Setting in Extension*

5 Would you reorder the underlined advantages of setting priorities according to your preference?

### Notes

1. clientele /ˌklaiən'tel/ *n.* customers collectively
2. phosphate /'fɔsˌfeit/ *n.* a salt of phosphoric acid
3. DDT   an insecticide that is also toxic to animals and humans; banned in the United States since 1972
4. zone /zəun/ *v.*   regulate housing in/of certain areas of towns

## A Critical Reader (II)

1 What do you know about the term "butterfly effect"? How is this term implicitly elaborated in this article?

2 How does this article, whose target readers are in the agricultural circle, influence your future planning?

## A Critical Writer

### I. Basic Writing Techniques

**1. Style and word choice**

1) As an argumentation, the theme of this article is to _____ its readers of the _____ of setting priorities, which is supported by _____ sub points, including _____, _____, _____, _____, and _____.

Since this article is written in an argumentative style, instead of persuasive, the word choice is to employ formal, accurate and emphatic words and expressions.

2) Word Replacement

Please read the following sentences extracted from this article, replace some expressions with original ones, and analyze the effect of the original expressions.

(1) If Extension is a problem-solving institution, and if Extension agents are indeed change agents, we must help people solve not only present needs and crises, but also problems of the future: ... (Paragraph 3)

(2) What we see as a cure may end up being worse than the disease. (Paragraph 8)

(3) We set priorities to get detailed results on important problems. These results will be noticed by those who demand we be reliable for our programs: ... (Paragraph 11)

(4) If we commit ourselves, and use our commitments to guide our activities, it will be easier for us to know what to do and when to do it. (Paragraph 13)

(5) All can work together on education for actions to reduce one intense community problem with terrible future consequences. (Paragraph 16)

## 2. Basic rules for good sentences and paragraphs

### 2.1 Basic rules

1) Unity

Please read the following sentences taken from different paragraphs, and see how several sentences have been united to serve as a common idea.

(1) How to deal with new technologies? What constitutes a healthy human being? How can we help people prepare for the changes the future will demand? (Paragraph 3)

(2) Extension priorities and our program priorities must not merely follow the trends of society. We must be in the advance guard of future problems, to prevent them before they occur or to help people meet them when they're inevitable. We must be flexible enough to respond to people's needs, but firm enough to stick with priorities and reach defined goals. (Paragraph 5)

(3) For instance, in light of predicted food shortages and high prices, an agricultural agent can plan programs to improve livestock production; a community development agent can concentrate on land use planning to save precious farm acreage; a home agent might program on low-cost nutrition; and a horticulture specialist could help people use home gardens as a supplement to store-bought food. (Paragraph 16)

2) Conciseness

Please paraphrase the following sentences, find out the figure of speech employed in these sentences, and tell the contribution these figures of speech make to sentence conciseness.

(1) Setting priorities and sticking to them is the only way to apply glue to a problem instead of a watery paste that spreads itself thin over many projects—and

wears off in a short time. (Paragraph 4)

(2) What we envision as a cure may end up being worse than the disease. (Paragraph 8)

(3) It will help us weigh risks and reduce uncertainty about the probability of future consequences occurring and thus make more rational decisions. (Paragraph 10)

(4) It helps those locked into traditional activities, by habit or demand, become more open to new and changing priority problems. (Paragraph 14)

(5) By so doing, we'll increase our impact, be more efficient and more credible, reach more people, help prevent crises, enjoy our work more, minimize risk and uncertainty, plan more realistically, keep our work up to date with changing needs, and use our resources more wisely. (Paragraph 17)

3) Cohesion and Coherence

Please read again Paragraphs 18 and 19, summarize this sub point, and make a judgment on the internal cohesion as well as its coherence with other sub points in this article.

**Priority setting helps our credibility and accountability.**

**Paragraph 18:** We set priorities to get concrete results on important problems. These results will be noticed by those who demand we be accountable for our programs: Extension administration, legislatures, the county board, our clientele, and our community.

**Paragraph 19:** More and more, people external to Extension are holding us accountable for program results they see as important. They ask: What are you doing? What do you have to show for the resources we've invested? What difference have you made in the lives of people you work with and for? Are your activities worth the tax dollars or grants provided to support them? Our credibility increases when we show results and measure up to what we've said our priorities are. If others help us set priorities and are aware of them, they can see how we meet those priorities. They'll see how we apply our resources to problems and "put our money where our mouth is." Successful activities build credibility, trust, and cooperation. Our credibility will be high only if we actually carry out actions other people can see, to meet goals they recognize as important.

**2.2 Exercise**

Please elaborate the following topic sentences with five to eight sentences and try to achieve paragraph unity.

1) The theory of evolution connects us to the natural world, explaining how and why we are a part of nature.

_____

_____

2) Change is the only thing that never changes.

_____

_____

3) Advanced technologies and science are the driving force behind the rich nations.

_____

_____

4) It's not the plan that is important, it's the planning.

_____
_____

### 3. Basic rules for good essays

#### 3.1 Unity of argumentation

Please read Paragraphs 1 and 17 again and find out how unity has been achieved.

**Paragraph 1:** There are many reasons to set priorities. Some are important to the clientele groups and larger society we serve; some are important for us to do our jobs well. These reasons fall into five categories:

**Paragraph 17:** Setting priorities as individuals and as an organization helps us aim our limited resources at the most critical problems. By so doing, we'll increase our impact, be more efficient and more credible, reach more people, help prevent crises, enjoy our work more, minimize risk and uncertainty, plan more realistically, keep our work up to date with changing needs, and use our resources more wisely. These are reasons why we need to set priorities.

In Paragraph 1, the first sentence states that _____; The second sentence divides the reasons into two types: _____ and _____; and the third sentence categorizes the reasons into five categories based on _____
_____.

In Paragraph 17, all reasons are _____ more specifically and a conclusion is consequently drawn, echoing the first paragraph.

#### 3.2 Working out an outline

Please draw a summary of this article, and make a judgment on its structural coherence.

## II. Specific Writing Techniques

### 1. Analysis of metaphorical effect

Please analyze sentences in this article which include metaphors, and share their effects on this argumentation.

### 2. Translation

Please put the following Chinese sentences which include metaphors into corresponding English ones.

1) 未来的帝国是心智的帝国。（丘吉尔）

_____

2) 变化是生命的不二法则。那些只懂得留恋过去或现在的人肯定将会错失未来。(肯尼迪)

_____

3) 目标是一场有期限的梦。（拿破仑·希尔）

4) 快乐并不是目标，它只是一个副产品。（罗斯福）

5) "任何人都可能食言，一切承诺都是浮云。"（莎士比亚）

## III. Your Turn to Write

Please try to write biographies as the following instructions say.
1. Please make a detailed five-year plan specific to months for yourself.
2. Write an argumentation to defend your above-made five-year plan with no less than 200 words.

### Pearls of Wisdom

1. I do not want to foresee the future. I am concerned with taking care of the present. God has given me no control over the moment following. —Mahatma Gandhi

2. Everyone here has the sense that right now is one of those moments when we are influencing the future. —Steve Jobs

3. A good plan violently executed now is better than a perfect plan executed next week. —George S. Patton

## Text C

### Warming up

1 How important do you feel an application letter will be for your future job hunting?
2 What are the necessary elements in an application letter?

### Application Letter

April 14, 2006
Mr. William Jackson
Employment Manager
Acme Pharmaceutical Corporation
13764 Jefferson Parkway
Roanoke, VA 24019
jackson@acmepharmaceutical.com

### A Critical Reader

1 Please list the top three sources for job seeking information?

Dear Mr. Jackson:

1. From your company's web site I learned about your need for a sales representative for the Virginia, Maryland, and North Carolina areas. I am very interested in this position with Acme Pharmaceuticals, and believe that my education and employment background are appropriate for the position.

2. While working toward my master's degree, I was employed as a sales representative with a small dairy foods firm. I increased my sales volume and profit margin appreciably while at Farmer's Foods, and I would like to repeat that success in the pharmaceutical industry. I have a strong academic background in biology and marketing, and think that I could apply my combination of knowledge and experience to the health industry. I will complete my master's degree in marketing in mid-May and will be available to begin employment in early June.

3. Enclosed is a copy of my <u>resume</u>, which more fully details my qualifications for the position.

4. I look forward to talking with you regarding sales opportunities with Acme Pharmaceuticals. <u>Within the next week I will contact you to confirm that you received my email and resumee and to answer any questions you may have</u>.

5. Thank you for your consideration.

Sincerely,
John Doe

[2] How much do you know about the difference between resumes and CVs?

[3] Is it appropriate to contact the recipients without getting their permission?

## A Critical Reader (II)

[1] After graduation, will you be confident enough to tell your future employers, as the author does in the beginning paragraph, that "I am very interested in this position with …, and believe that my education and employment background are appropriate for the position"?

[2] Please introduce the origin of the term "John Doe" to your classmates.

# A Critical Writer

## I. Writing An Application/Recommendation Letter

### 1. Style and basic elements

A letter of application, also known as a _____ _____, is a document sent with one's _____ to provide additional information on one's skills and experience.

A letter of application typically provides detailed information on _____ one is qualified for the job he/she is applying for. Effective application letters explain the reasons for one's _____ in the specific organization and identify one's most relevant _____ or _____.

One's application letter should let the employer know what _____ one is applying for, why the employer should select the person for an interview, and how the writer will follow-up.

### 2. General structure

• First Paragraph: Why writing—mention the job applied for and where the listing is found.

• Middle Paragraph(s): What can be offered to the employer? Mention why one's skills and experiences are a good fit for the job.

• Last Paragraph: "thank you" to the hiring manager for considering the applicant and note how one will follow up.

### 3. Format

*Contact Information*

Name
Address
City, State, Zip Code
Phone Number
Email Address

Date
Employer Contact Information (*if you have it*)
Name
Title
Company
Address
City, State, Zip Code

*Salutation*

Dear Mr./Ms. Last Name, (*leave out if you don't have a contact*)

*Body of Application Letter*

First Paragraph

The first paragraph of an application letter should include information on why the applicant is writing. Mention the job he/she is applying for and where he/she found the job listing. Include the name of a mutual contact, if he/she has one.

Middle Paragraph(s)

The next section of an application letter should describe what the applicant has to offer the employer. Mention specifically how his/her qualifications match the job he/she applying for. (Remember, the applicant is interpreting his/her resume, not repeating it.)

Final Paragraph

Conclude the application letter by thanking the employer for considering the applicant for the position. Include information on how he/she will follow-up.

*Complimentary Close*

Sincerely,
*Signature*

### 4. Exercises

1) Please find out as much information as possible about both the applicant and the position he/she is applying for.

Dear Contact Person:

I'm writing to express my interest in the Web Content Specialist position listed on Monster.com. I have experience building large, consumer-focused health-based content sites. While much of my experience has been in the business world, I understand the social value of the non-profit sector and my business experience will be an asset to your organization.

My responsibilities included the development and management of the site's editorial voice and style, the editorial calendar, and the daily content programming and production of the web site. I worked closely with health care professionals and medical editors to help them provide the best possible information to a consumer audience of patients. In addition, I helped physicians learn to utilize their medical content to write user-friendly, readily comprehensible text.

Experience has taught me how to build strong relationships with all departments at an organization. I have the ability to work within a team as well as cross-team. I can work with web engineers to resolve technical issues and implement technical enhancements, work with the development department to implement design and functional enhancements, and monitor site statistics and conduct search engine optimization.

Thank you for your consideration.

Chapter Nine   Future Plans

*Laura Stanley*

2) Please follow the model Recommendation Letter below to write one employment reference for the applicant, Laura Stanley, in the exercise above based on her details. Your assumed identity would be one of the health care professionals she once worked with.

*Defenition of Employment References*—A professional recommendation letter given for _____ reasons is best done so by a boss or supervisor. They should provide an overall analysis of the _____ of the individual. This letter should save the future _____ the time and trouble of calling to do a reference check.

>
> Your Name
> Your Address
> Your City, State, Zip Code
> Your Phone Number
> Your Email Address
>
> Date
>
> To whom it may concern:
>
> I would like to recommend Muriel MacKensie as a candidate for a position with your organization. In her position as Adminstrative Assistant, Muriel was employed in our office from 2004 - 2008.
>
> Muriel did an excellent job in this position and was an asset to our organization during her tenure with the office. She has excellent written and verbal communication skills, is extremely organized, can work independently, and is able to effectly multi-task to ensure that all projects are completed in a timely manner.
>
> Muriel was always willing to offer her assistance and had an excellent rapport with the many constituents served by our office including clients, employers, and other professional organizations. She would be an asset to any employer and I recommend her for any endeavor she chooses to pursue.
>
> Yours truly,
>
> *Handwritten Signature* (mailed letter)
>
> Typed Signature

To whom it may concern:

I would like to recommend Laura Stanley, ...

_____
_____
_____
_____
_____
_____

Yours truly,

_____

Typed Signature

## II. Your Turn to Write an Essay

Please write an application letter for the post below. All your educational and working experiences are listed out in the chart for your reference.

*Post:*

Management Trainee in Wong And Lim Consulting

Advertised on the Student Affairs Office notice board of the Hong Kong Polytechnic University on 23 July 2012.

*Educational Background:*

studying a B.A. in Management at the Hong Kong Polytechnic University

graduating in 2013

*Subjects Learned:*

Operations Management, Human Resources Management, Accounting, Marketing and Strategic Management.

final year project is entitled Knowledge Management Practices in HK

*Skills:*

fluent spoken and written English

fluent spoken and written Mandarin

*Working Experiences:*

held the post of Executive in the Management Society

practiced in Lucky Star Garment Manufactory Limited

## Pearls of Wisdom

1. All labor that uplifts humanity has dignity and importance and should be undertaken with painstaking excellence.　　　　—Martin Luther King, Jr.

2. Be regular and orderly in your life, so that you may be violent and original in your work.　　　　—Gustave Flaubert

3. Far and away the best prize that life has to offer is the chance to work hard at work worth doing.　　　　—Theodore Roosevelt

Chapter Nine  Future Plans

# Corpus-based Exercises (9)

## I. Key Word: plan

**1.** *Plan* is one of the key words in this chapter. Please categorize the collocations of *plan* into the following categories.

| | | | |
|---|---|---|---|
| highly-educated executives who can | plan | and analyze to beat the band but w | |
| t happens in life is a result of a grand | plan | or destiny . / 2 . American Value : C | |
| king can do to good brands . A marketing | plan | centred on discounts and promotions | |
| njury . / Carson came up with a | plan | to give both twins the best chance of | |
| ife without an externally supported daily | plan | can lead to higher rates of dru | 5 |
| his intelligent 22-year-old announced a | plan | for a party , the guests to include a v | |
| atter how carefully I plan my time , the | plan | always goes wrong . / If I create sch | |
| . The old saying that you " get what you | plan | for " is so true . Your dream won't ju | |
| need to sit down , on a regular basis , and | plan | out your strategy for achieving the d | |
| rough all of the details . Break the whole | plan | down into small , workable parts . T | 10 |
| ey sensibly . Here are some ideas : /— | Plan | ahead . /—Sit down , and write | |
| ouse down . / Fortunately , a survival | plan | was drawn up by the Yemeni govern | |
| efore . In just two years , the international | plan | against AIDS has grown from ideas | |
| uch thought , I came up with a brilliant | plan | for Rich to meet my mother and win | |
| lways so easy . Even young students who | plan | on staying in the United States just l | 15 |
| even . When he finally retired , he put his | plan | into effect . / Three or four days afte | |
| t an age when I had a career , a long-term | plan | and a more or less settled life ( and n | |
| thought , I came up with a brilliant | plan | . I worked out a way for Rich to mee | |
| ents can be very satisfying , too , if you | plan | far enough in advance and really thi | |
| question to ask is : how can an optimum | plan | be worked out to deal effectively wit | 20 |
| r mind 's eye a heavenly vision , a precise | plan | , that is so great , so perfect , it can't | |
| enefits it is important to devise a backup | plan | . Individuals who assume that their | |
| arket in the year 2000 , and one tentative | plan | is to use the Internet to transmit info | |
| Jan . 10 , the European Union unveiled a | plan | to cut energy use across the continen | |
| t away . / It was not really a conscious | plan | that Marlboro made to hoist himself | 25 |

**plan** *n.*
A. + plan _____
N. + plan _____
V. (Verbal Phrases) + plan _____

V. + plan + Compl. _____

plan + V. _____

plan + Prep. _____

**plan** *v.*

plan and V. _____

plan + Prep. _____

plan + Adv. _____

**2. Please employ the appropriate forms of the above-listed "plan"-related expressions to translate the following Chinese sentences into English.**

1) 在管理学中，计划具有两重含义，其一是计划工作……

_____

_____

2) 他开始缓慢但细致地制订他的"飞天"计划。

_____

_____

3) 他们喜欢有序的生活，希望一切都按计划开展。

_____

_____

4) 如果你打算去国外用你的"黑莓"或者"苹果"手机，你得弄清楚这个想法能不能通过海外接收数据而得以实施。

_____

_____

5) 一个能够按期推进工作进程的经理人是值得信赖的。对于一家公司而言，他的价值远远高于那些雄心万丈、学识渊博但毫无执行力的管理人员。

_____

_____

## II. Key Word: future.

| | | |
|---|---|---|
| s ? 500 ? 1000 ? Will it be **a technological** | future | with space hotels , rocket cars , ge |
| utomated homes ? Or will it be **an organic** | future | with a new emphasis on spirituality an |
| their minds for **a highly competitive** | future | ? The first step , say experts , is to cre |
| presenting the moment when **the real** | future | begins . / In less than six years tha |
| as talking about pre-emptively **striking** | future | foes like Iraq . But Bush was also p     5 |
| ideo-game—and , in some not too **distant** | future | , the hand-held cell-phone or person |
| de who will be inspired by **the unimagined** | future | made possible by the global coopera |
| r abroad—**a cashless , digital-money** | future | may be fast approaching . / T |
| r contributions to humanity and to **a better** | future | for yourselves and the generations th |
| is unlikely to go there anytime in **the near** | future | , because no Palestinian can venture    10 |

| | | |
|---|---|---|
| ciety , and they are angry about their **empty** | future | . / So this is a very pregnant mome |
| er their sons and daughters toward **a secure** | future | . But the sons and daughters want to m |
| Creativity is the key to **a brighter** | future | , say education and business expert |
| ue personality and with **a very different** | future | awaiting her . Yet , although eac |
| " silver lining " appeared in **the cloudy** | future | of the Does . A popular TV show    15 |
| er their sons and daughters toward **a secure** | future | . But the sons and daughters wan |
| ortant . They try to show the many **possible** | future | that lie open to us . / For the |
| alization can be seen as a sign of **a hopeful** | future | by some . By others this is a disa |
| ant to buy a cheap house with **an uncertain** | future | , apply to a house agent in one o |
| use . They see a day in **the not-too-distant** | future | when all autos will be abandone    20 |
| ng means of urban travel in **the foreseeable** | future | . / The motorcar will undoubte |
| be better able to provide **a secure financial** | future | for their 7-year-old grandson . / |
| porters . They face the front , **the absolute** | future | , without any hesitation . Rab know |
| n had said . ' You have to build **a different** | future | . Not one that revolves around thi |
| l ; to preparation for **a more or less remote** | future | is opposed making the most of the op    25 |
| lieve one acute community problem with **dire** | future | consequences . Such coordination in p |

**All collocations of *future* listed above are in the "A. + future" style. Please translate all of the boldfaced nominal phrases into Chinese.**

# Chapter Ten

# Controversial Issues

### Warming up

1  Morality refers to a set of values or codes of conduct that are accepted by people in a society to distinguish right from wrong. It contributes significantly to forming our ethical standards; hence, a certain level of moral awareness is generally expected from everyone in a society. In recent years however, we discover that the public has sometimes shown considerable coldness towards those who are in desperate need of help. Such phenomena are considered to be the result of moral apathy.

2  Work with a partner and discuss the following questions. What do you think is moral apathy? Can you illustrate your point by two specific examples? What has caused moral apathy? Make a list of some possible causes.

## Text A

### Civilized Society Distorted by Moral Apathy[1]

By Yvonne Brill (chinadaily.com.cn)

1. One characteristic of a civilized society is that it shows evidence of moral and intellectual advancement, and can be described using adjectives such as humane, ethical, and reasonable. It would stand to reason then, that individuals living within a civilized society would exhibit the same attributes[2]. Surely it is humane, ethical, and reasonable to lend a hand to fellow civilians in their time of need. But history, and many contemporary examples, shows us that, at times, individuals shy away from humane or ethical reactions, and further towards that of self-interest or apathy.

2. A recent example from China is that of a two-year-old girl in the city of Foshan in Guangdong province who was hit by two vehicles after wandering onto the road.

### A Critical Reader (I)

1  What purpose does the first paragraph serve?

2  Please identify the structural elements of the first paragraph.

3  What functions do Paragraphs 2, 3 and 4 perform?

The girl lay unconscious and bleeding on the ground for six minutes as over a dozen people passed her body, none of whom stopped to check on her or help. The incident was captured by a surveillance camera, and has sparked an outcry from Chinese media and netizens alike, decrying[3] the lack of morals of a society that would pass by an individual in need, a child no less, without attempting to help in some way.

3. Other examples from China include a woman who was stabbed by her own son at Shanghai's Pudong International Airport where video footage, uploaded to the internet, showed a group of people standing by watching as the woman lay on the ground, and the only person attempting to help her was a laowai (foreigner), who crouched beside her, applying pressure to her stab wounds. Another news report tells of an elderly man in Central China's Hubei province who collapsed in a marketplace and was left to lie facedown for an hour and half until family members arrived to take him to the hospital. He later died.

4. But is it a lack of morals that feeds apathy or spurs passersby to keep on walking, or something more? Some may cite the social psychological phenomenon of "bystander effect", which theorizes that the probability of receiving help is inversely related to the number of bystanders. That is, the more people who witness an event, the less likely any one individual will provide help. Others, especially those in China familiar with the case of Peng Yu, may consider the fear of repercussions[4] as a result of offering aid to be a more likely root cause.

5. The 2006 case of Peng Yu is widely considered to have "damaged society" in China, resulting in citizens becoming increasingly wary of lending a hand to strangers in need. Peng Yu, a young resident of Nanjing, Jiangsu province, came to the aid of an elderly woman who had fallen in a public area. The women later accused him of causing her fall, and took him to court. The court decided in favor of the woman based on the "common sense" reasoning that Peng would not have helped the woman had he not felt guilt from causing the fall in the first place, and ordered him to pay compensation of 40,000 Yuan.

6. The phenomenon of fearing repercussions from volunteering help is not unique to China though, and other countries have enacted civil laws known as "Good

Samaritan"⁵ laws for this very reason. America, known for its <u>litigious</u> culture, has laws designed to protect those who voluntarily come to the aid of those in need from repercussions such as being sued or prosecuted for wrongful death or unintentional injury. Canada also has laws that protect those who volunteer aid from liability⁶.

7. <u>While the laws in North America focus on removing liability from Good Samaritans, some countries in Europe have laws that instead criminalize failure to help, focusing on citizens' "duty to rescue"</u>. Examples from Europe include France's law that refers to deliberately failing to provide assistance to a person in danger, and Germany's law that obliges a citizen to provide help in the event of an accident or general danger, and Serbia's law that requires citizens to provide help to anyone in need as long as it does not place them in danger personally. In my own country, New Zealand, it is a crime to fail to report child abuse—citizens are now legally obliged with a "duty to report", whereby it is an offence to fail to take reasonable steps to protect a child from the risk of death, grievous bodily hard, or sexual assault.

8. It is sad that some modern societies require laws to spur members of those societies to act in moral way, which, in my opinion, is the basis of our very humanity. I find it hard to believe that each and every person who passed the young hit-and-run victim as she lay injured in the street was fearful of possible repercussions for volunteering help. Rather, it seems a mix of moral apathy, a lack of social trust in the legal system, and an increasingly declining sense of community is at work to produce the kind of society where vulnerable members can be left without help in their time of need.

9. Acting in a humane, ethical, reasonable and moral way is at the basis of a civilized society where civilians know the difference between right and wrong. What is acceptable and what is not acceptable. <u>In order to maintain this kind society it is imperative that the actions of citizens of any country, not just China, be judged against a scale of right and wrong in relation to humane, ethical, reasonable and moral behavior</u>. In this case, the behavior of citizens who passed an injured child in the street without offering help falls squarely into the category of inhumane, unethical, unreasonable

**4** In your opinion, which approach will be more effective in China, "Good Samaritan" laws or punishment for failure to help?

**5** In Paragraph 8, the author presents her understanding of what has caused people's coldness toward those who are in need of help. Do you agree with her analysis? Why or why not?

and immoral, and therefore weakens the foundation of civilized society.

> **Notes**
>
> 1. apathy /'æpəθi/ *n.*  lack of interest, enthusiasm or concern; indifference
> 2. attribute /'ætrɪbjuːt/ *n.*  quality regarded as a natural or typical part of sb/sth
> 3. decry /dɪ'kraɪ/ *v.*  to condemn openly.
> 4. repercussion /riːpə'kʌʃən/ *n.*  [C usu. pl] indirect effect or result (esp unpleasant) of an event, etc;
> 5. Samaritan /sə'mærətn/ *n.*  (idm) a good Samaritan a person who gives sympathy and help to people in trouble
> 6. liability /laɪə'bɪlɪti/ *n.*  legal responsibility for something, especially for paying money that is owed, or for damage or injury

## A Critical Reader (II)

In your opinion, to eradicate moral apathy among us, what should the government as well as the people do? Make a list of at list three suggestions.

## A Critical Writer

### I. Basic Writing Techniques

#### 1. Style and word choice

**1.1 Consider the following questions:**

1) Think about the four levels of diction described in the introduction section of this book. Which level of diction does this article adopt? What kind of writing style does the author follow (formal vs. informal)?

2) How is the writing style reflected through the word choice? Support your opinion by locating from the article ten examples of word choice that are consistent with the writing style.

e.g.

(1) It would stand to reason then, that individuals living within a civilized society would **exhibit** the same **attributes**. (Paragraph 1)

(2) The phenomenon of fearing **repercussions** from volunteering help is not **unique** to China though, and other countries have enacted civil laws known as "Good Samaritan" laws for this very reason. (Paragraph 3)

(3) In my own country, New Zealand, it is a crime to fail to report child abuse—citizens are now **legally obliged with** a "duty to report", **whereby** it is an offence to fail to take reasonable steps to protect a child from the risk of death, grievous bodily hard, or sexual assault. (Paragraph 7)

1.2　When we read, we often encounter new words, but it does not mean that we have to look up every new word in the dictionary. Being able to guess the meaning of a word with the help of the context information is an important reading strategy. Write down five words you do not know in this article. Write down the meaning of them you guess and then look up the words in the dictionary to check if you have guessed correctly.

| Words you do not know | Meanings you guess | Dictionary definitions of the words |
|---|---|---|
|  |  |  |
|  |  |  |
|  |  |  |
|  |  |  |
|  |  |  |

1.3　Diction: change the underlying words and expressions with the ones from the text.

The phenomenon of fearing <u>long-lasting bad effects</u> from volunteering help is not unique to China though, and other countries have enacted civil laws known as "Good <u>People</u>" laws for this very reason. America, known for its culture that is <u>very willing to take disagreements to a court of law</u>, has laws designed to protect those who voluntarily come to the aid of those in need from repercussions such as being sued or <u>officially accused</u> for wrongful death or unintentional injury. Canada also has laws that protect those who volunteer aid from <u>legal responsibility</u>. (Paragraph 6)

**Key:** The phenomenon of fearing <u>repercussions</u> from volunteering help is not unique to China though, and other countries have enacted civil laws known as "Good <u>Samaritan</u>" laws for this very reason. America, known for its <u>litigious</u> culture, has laws designed to protect those who voluntarily come to the aid of those in need from repercussions such as being sued or <u>prosecuted</u> for wrongful death or unintentional injury. Canada also has laws that protect those who volunteer aid from <u>liability</u>.

## 2. Basic Rules for Good Sentences

### 2.1　Unity: one single, complete thought.

Please read the following sentences and try to find out how unity is displayed:

One characteristic of a civilized society is that it shows evidence of moral and intellectual advancement, and can be described using adjectives such as humane, ethical, and reasonable. It would stand to reason then, that individuals living within a civilized society would exhibit the same attributes. (Paragraph 1)

**Analysis:** Sentence 1 presents the author's opinion of what kind of society can be considered as civilized. Sentence 2 develops this idea and points out individuals in such a society should thus demonstrate the qualities mentioned in sentence 1. Clearly, sentence 2 builds on sentence 1 and develops it. They are both united under the same idea.

**2.2 Coherence: clear connection between parts; no faulty parallel constructions, no unknown pronouns, no unclear relationships.**

Please read the following sentences and try to find out how coherence is displayed:

Some may cite the social psychological phenomenon of "bystander effect", which theorizes that the probability of receiving help is inversely related to the number of bystanders. That is, the more people who witness an event, the less likely any one individual will provide help. (Paragraph 4)

**Analysis:** The first part of the sentence introduces the concept "bystander effect", and the second part explains it in an adjective clause. The word "which" refers back to that concept and helps the logical flow of ideas. The second sentence further clarifies the concept in different words, using "that is" to indicate the connection between these two sentences. The concept is the thread that runs through the two sentences. The second sentence builds on the first on and logically develops it.

**2.3 Conciseness: no unnecessary words.**

Read the following sentence and analyze how conciseness is accomplished.

e.g.

In my own country, New Zealand, it is a crime to fail to report child abuse – citizens are now legally obliged with a 'duty to report', whereby it is an offence to fail to take reasonable steps to protect a child from the risk of death, grievous bodily hard, or sexual assault. (Paragraph 7)

**Analysis:** The word "whereby" is very well used. By using this word, the author avoids unnecessary repetition of previously mentioned information and makes the sentence terse.

**2.4 Imitation**

Make your own sentences by simulating the structure of the given sentences. For each sentence, pay attention to the words in bold face.

(1) That is, **the more** people who witness an event, **the less** likely any one individual will provide help.

_____

(2) The phenomenon of fearing repercussions from volunteering help is not unique to China.

_____

(3) **While the laws in North America** focus on removing liability from Good Samaritans, **some countries in Europe** have laws that instead criminalize failure to help, focusing on citizens' "duty to rescue".

(4) **In order to** maintain this kind society **it is imperative that** the actions of citizens of any country, not just China, be judged against a scale of right and wrong in relation to humane, ethical, reasonable and moral behavior.

### 3. Basic Rules for Good Paragraphs

3.1  Please read Paragraph 7 and discuss how unity is displayed in this paragraph by doing the following things: first, identify the main idea of the paragraph; next, discuss how this idea is developed in this paragraph.

3.2  Analysis

1) Unity:

This paragraph displays good unity. The first sentence identifies the controlling idea of the paragraph: European countries approach the issue of volunteering help from the angle of citizens' duty to rescue. The rest of the paragraph provides specific examples to support this idea. All the examples are relevant to the topic and give powerful support to the controlling idea.

2) Coherence:

The coherence of a paragraph or article is accomplished through various means, among which logical transitions play a critical role. There are two types of transitions: within paragraph transitions and between paragraph transitions. **Within paragraph transitions** are usually made by using **conjunctive adverbs** and **transitional phrases**. Properly used, these adverbs and phrases can make clear the logical relations between two sentences, allowing ideas flow smoothly in the paragraph. Below are some examples of them:

**Conjunctive adverbs:** *therefore, however, although, meanwhile, accordingly, undoubtedly.*

**Transitional phrases:** *in addition, for example, as a result, in contrast, on the contrary, in other words.*

It has to be pointed out that not every transition is made through conjunctive adverbs or transitional phrases. Sometimes repeating or referring back to a term or concept appeared in the previous sentence, can make the logical connection clear; so it is important that we do not overwhelm the reader with excessive conjunctive adverbs and transitional phrases.

Between paragraph transitions are often achieved by putting a transitional sentence at the beginning of the paragraph that connects the paragraph with the previous one.

Paragraph 7 displays good coherence.

**While the laws in North America focus on removing liability from Good Samaritans, some countries in Europe have laws that instead criminalize failure to help, focusing on citizens' "duty to rescue". Examples from Europe** include France's **law** that refers to deliberately failing to provide assistance to a person in danger, and Germany's **law** that obliges a citizen to provide help in the event of an accident or general danger, and Serbia's **law** that requires citizens to provide help to anyone in need as long as it does not place them in danger personally. In my own country, New Zealand, it is a **crime** to fail to report child abuse—citizens are now legally obliged with a "duty to report", whereby it is an offence to fail to take reasonable steps to protect a child from the risk of death, grievous bodily hard, or sexual assault.

**Analysis:** In the previous paragraph (Paragraph 6), the author introduces laws in the U.S. regarding the issue of volunteering help. This paragraph begins with a transitional topic sentence that indicates the connection between the present paragraph with the previous one and leads smoothly to the main idea of this paragraph: how the European countries approach the issue. The transition makes the progress of ideas smooth and natural. In the rest of the paragraph, the author begins by "examples include…" to show that what follow are examples of the idea just expressed. In addition, the word "law" is repeated three times in different examples and the word "crime" is used in the last to show that the examples are all related to the same topic, tightly united under the same controlling idea; thus the logical connection between the sentences are made transparent and the ideas flow very naturally in the whole paragraph, making the paragraph coherent.

### 3.3 Exercise

Please read Paragraphs 1 and 2. Identify the transitional strategies as well as all the specific transitional devices that are employed by the author.

### 3.4 Working out an outline

In your opinion, to eradicate moral apathy among us, what should the government as well as the people do? At the end of this section, you will be asked to write an article on this topic. Now, think carefully about this topic and write a working outline of your essay. Your writing plan should address at least the following questions:

1) How many parts and paragraphs do you plan to write?
2) What is the main idea for each paragraph?
3) What kind of details will you use to support the topic sentence of each body paragraph?

## 4. Basic Rule for Good Essays: Well-organized Structure

**4.1** Please briefly describe the structure of this essay.

**4.2 Analysis:**

This essay is well-organized, with a clear structure.

**Part one (Paragraph 1):** the lead-in

1) **Paragraph 1** is the introduction section of the article. It opens the discussion by an argument and some reasoning, which introduces the topic and thesis of the article. The tone of the whole text is set in this part as well.

Part two (Paragraph 2—8): the development

2) **Paragraph 2 and 3** describes two recent events happened in China to provide more background information on the topic and prepare the reader for the discussion that follows.

3) **Paragraph 4** presents two current views on the possible causes for moral apathy in China and Paragraph 5 describes another event happened a few years ago as support for the second possible cause "fear of repercussions".

4) In **Paragraph 6 and 7**, the author describes how American and European countries deal with the issue of volunteering help to avoid moral apathy.

5) In **paragraph 8** the author comments on the issue of moral apathy and expresses her opinion on the cause of moral apathy.

Part three (Paragraph 9): the end-conclusion

6) In **Paragraph 9** the author reiterates her opinion on this issue and puts an end to the discussion.

## II. Special Writing Techniques

### 1. Supporting your argument by providing specific examples

In paragraph development, it is important that you convey your ideas accurately and clearly so that the reader can have a good understanding of the exact meaning. Often, your point is made clear by providing evidential support. Effective support will validate your argument while insufficient support will weaken your point. Support is generally divided into four categories: factual, logical, statistical and anecdotal support.

Factual support: facts, events actually happened, and truth etc.

Logical support: logical analysis or reasoning.

Statistical support: statistics gained from investigation or research.

Anecdotal support: anecdotes, e.g. a story you hear, etc. It is less reliable than other sorts of support and thus does not carry the weight of authority. This type of evidence is not acceptable in research papers and other papers that require scientific evidence.

### 2. Read Paragraph 7 and think about how factual evidence is used in the paragraph to support the controlling idea of the topic sentence.

**Analysis:** In this paragraph, the author provides three pieces of factual evidence to support her point. This evidence can be acquired by doing some research, because they are true, they are often very convincing.

### 3. Write a paragraph based on the topic sentence given below.

Make sure your paragraph has concrete support, good unity and coherence. You might want to do some research to obtain necessary supporting evidence.

Volunteering help should not bring about any negative consequences.

___

## III. Your Turn to Write

In your opinion, to eradicate moral apathy among us, what should the government as well as the people do? Present your opinion in a well-organized essay. Make sure your essay has effective support, unity and coherence.

## Pearls of Wisdom

1. Apathy is a sort of living oblivion. —Horace Greeley

2. Apathy can be overcome by enthusiasm, and enthusiasm can only be aroused by two things: first, an ideal, with takes the imagination by storm, and second, a definite intelligible plan for carrying that ideal into practice.
—Arnold J. Toynbee

3. Hate is not the opposite of love; apathy is. —Rollo May

4. I have a very strong feeling that the opposite of love is not hate—it's apathy. It's not giving a damn. —Leo Buscaglia

5. People have moved beyond apathy, beyond skepticism into deep cynicism.
—Elliot Richardson

6. Persecution was at least a sign of personal interest. Tolerance is composed of nine parts of apathy to one of brotherly love. —Frank Moore Colby

7. The apathy of the people is enough to make every statue leap from its pedestal and hasten the resurrection of the dead. —William Lloyd Garrison

8. Tolerance it a tremendous virtue, but the immediate neighbors of tolerance are apathy and weakness. —James Goldsmith

# Text B

## Warming up

1. There have been long-lasting debates on whether the death penalty should be abolished or not. Both people who support it and those who oppose it have well-grounded arguments. Work with a partner and fill in the following chart with some of their arguments?

| Arguments for the death penalty | Arguments against the death penalty |
|---|---|
|  |  |
|  |  |
|  |  |
|  |  |
|  |  |
|  |  |

2. What is your opinion on the death penalty? Share it with a partner and explain why you take that position.

## Death and Justice

by Edward I. Koch

### A Critical Reader (I)

1. Last December a man named Robert Lee Willie, who had been convicted of raping and murdering an 18-year-old woman, was executed in the Louisiana state prison. In a statement issued several minutes before his death, Mr. Willie said: "Killing people is wrong... It makes no difference whether it's citizens, countries, or governments. Killing is wrong." Two weeks later in South Carolina, an admitted killer named Joseph Carl Shaw was put to death for murdering two teenagers. In an appeal to the governor for clemency[1], Mr. Shaw wrote: "Killing is wrong when I did it. Killing is wrong when you do it. I hope you have the courage and moral

[1] How does the author introduce the topic of this article? What do you think are his reasons for choosing this particular method?

strength to stop the killing."

2. It is a curiosity of modern life that we find ourselves being lectured on morality by cold-blooded killers. Mr. Willie previously had been convicted of aggravated[2] rape, aggravated kidnapping, and the murders of a Louisiana deputy and a man from Missouri. Mr. Shaw committed another murder a week before the two for which he was executed, and admitted mutilating[3] the body of the 14-year-old girl he killed. I can't help wondering what prompted these murderers to speak out against killing as they entered the death-house door. Did their newfound reverence[4] for life stem from the realization that they were about to lose their own?

3. Life is indeed precious, and I believe the death penalty helps to affirm this fact. Had the death penalty been a real possibility in the minds of these murderers, they might well have stayed their hand. They might have shown moral awareness before their victims died, and not after. Consider the tragic death of Rosa Velez, who happened to be home when a man named Luis Vera burglarized[5] her apartment in Brooklyn. "Yeah, I shot her," Vera admitted. "She knew me, and I knew I wouldn't go to the chair".

4. During my 22 years in public service, I have heard the pros and cons of capital punishment expressed with special intensity. As a district leader, councilman, congressman, and mayor, I have represented constituencies generally thought of as liberal. Because I support the death penalty for heinous[6] crimes for murder, I have sometimes been the subject of emotional and outraged attacks by voters who find my position reprehensible[7] or worse. I have listened to their ideas. I have weighed their objections carefully. I still support the death penalty. The reasons I maintain my position can be best understood by examining the arguments most frequently heard in opposition.

5. (1) The death penalty is "barbaric." Sometimes opponents of capital punishment horrify with tales of lingering[8] death on the gallows[9], of faulty electric chairs, or of agony in the gas chamber. Partly in response to such protests, several states such as North Carolina and Texas switched to execution by lethal[10] injection. The condemned person is put to death painlessly, without ropes, voltage, bullets, or gas. Did this answer the

**2** How does the author plan to argue for his position? Do you think it is an effective way to make his point? Why or why not?

**3** Is there any other method the author could use to argue for his position?

objections of death penalty opponents. Of course not. On June 22, 1984, *The New York Times* published an editorial that sarcastically attacked the new "hygienic" method of death by injection, and stated that "execution can never be made humane through science." So it's not the method that really troubles opponents. It's the death itself they consider barbaric.

6. Admittedly, capital punishment is not a pleasant topic. However, one does not have to like the death penalty in order to support it any more than one must like radical surgery, radiation, or chemotherapy[11] in order to find necessary these attempts at curing cancer. Ultimately we may learn how to cure cancer with a simple pill. Unfortunately, that day has not yet arrived. Today we are faced with the choice of letting the cancer spread or trying to cure it with the methods available, methods that one day will almost certainly be considered barbaric. But to give up and do nothing would be far more barbaric and would certainly delay the discovery of an eventual cure. The analogy between cancer and murder is imperfect, because murder is not the "disease" we are trying to cure. The disease is injustice. We may not like the death penalty, but it must be available to punish crimes of cold-blooded murder, cases in which any other form of punishment would be inadequate and, therefore, unjust. If we create a society in which injustice is not tolerated, incidents of murder—the most flagrant[12] form of injustice—will diminish.

7. (2) No other major democracy uses the death penalty. No other major democracy—in fact, few other countries of any description—are plagued by a murder rate such as that in the United States. Fewer and fewer Americans can remember the days when unlocked doors were the norm and murder was a rare and terrible offense. In America the murder rate climbed 122 percent between 1963 and 1980. During the same period, the murder rate in New York City increased by almost 400 percent, and the statistics are even worse in many other cities. A study at M.I.T showed that based on 1970 homicide[13] rates a person who lived in a large American city ran a greater risk of being murdered than an American soldier in World War, ran of being killed in combat. It is not surprising that the laws of each country

[4] According to the author, how is injustice like cancer? Do you agree with the author's analogy?

[5] Is the death penalty an effective way to make sure convicted killers do not kill again? Are there any other methods that can achieve this purpose?

differ according to differing conditions and traditions. If other countries had our murder problem, the cry for capital punishment would be just as loud as it is here. And I daresay that any other major democracy where 75 percent of the people supported the death penalty would soon enact it into law.

8. (3) An innocent person might be executed by mistake. Consider the work of Adam Bedau, one of the most implacable foes of capital punishment in this country. According to Mr. Bedau, it is "false sentimentality[14] to argue that the death penalty should be abolished because of the abstract possibility that an innocent person might be executed." He cites a study of the 7,000 executions in this country from 1893 to 1971, and concludes that the record fails to show that such cases occur. The main point, however, is this. If government functioned only when the possibility of error didn't exist, government wouldn't function at all. Human life deserves special protection, and one of the best ways to guarantee that protection is to assure that convicted murderers do not kill again. Only the death penalty can accomplish this end. In a recent case in New Jersey, a man named Richard Biegenwald was freed from prison after serving 18 years for murder; since his release he has been convicted of committing four murders. A prisoner named Lemuel Smith, who, while serving four life sentences for murder (plus two life sentences for kidnapping and robbery) in New York's Green Haven Prison, lured a woman corrections officer into the chaplain's office and strangled[15] her. He then mutilated and dismembered her body. An additional life sentence for Smith is meaningless. Because New York has no death penalty statute[16], Smith has effectively been given a license to kill.

9. But the problem of multiple murder is not confined to the nation's penitentiaries[17]. In 1981, 91 police officers were killed in the line of duty in this country. Seven percent of those arrested in the cases that have been solved had a previous arrest for murder. In New York City in 1976 and 1977, 85 persons arrested for homicide had a previous arrest for murder. Six of these individuals had two previous arrests for murder, and one had four previous murder arrests. During those two years the New York police were arresting for murder

persons with a previous arrest for murder on the average of one every 8.5 days. This is not surprising when we learn that in 1975, for example, the median time served in Massachusetts for homicide was less than two-and-a-half years. In 1976, a study sponsored by the Twentieth Century Fund found that the average time served in the United States for first-degree murder is ten years. The median time served may be considerably lower.

10. (4) Capital punishment cheapens the value of human life. On the contrary, it can be easily demonstrated that death penalty strengthens the value of human life. If the penalty for rape were lowered, clearly it would signal a lessened regard for the victims' suffering, humiliation, and personal integrity. It would cheapen their horrible experience, and expose them to an increase danger of recurrence. When we lower the penalty for murder, it signals a lessened regard for the values of the victim's life. Some critics of capital punishment, such as columnist Jimmy Breslin, have suggested that a life sentence is actually a harsher penalty for murder than death. This is sophistic[18] nonsense. A few killers may decide not to appeal a death sentence, but the overwhelming majority make every effort to stay alive. It is by exacting the highest penalty for the taking of human life that we affirm the highest value of human life.

11. (5) The death penalty is applied in a discriminatory manner. This factor no longer seems to be the problem it once was. The appeals process for a condemned prisoner is lengthy and painstaking. Every effort is made to see that the verdict and sentence were fairly arrived at. However, assertions of discrimination are not an argument for ending the death penalty but for extending it. It is not justice to exclude everyone from the penalty of the law if a few are found to be so favored. Justice requires that the law be applied equally to all.

12. (6) Thou Shalt Not Kill. The Bible is our greatest source of moral inspiration. Opponents of the death penalty frequently cite the sixth of the Ten Commandments in an attempt to prove that capital punishment is divinely proscribed[19]. In the original Hebrew, however, the Sixth Commandment reads, "Thou shalt Not Commit Murder", and the Torah specifies capital punishment for a variety of offenses. The biblical

6 Do you think that the death penalty is applied in a discriminatory manner in our country? If so, should we abolish the death penalty?

viewpoint has been upheld by philosophers throughout history. The greatest thinker of the 19th century—Kant[20], Locke[21], Hobbes[22], Rousseau[23], Montesquieu[24], and Mill[25]—agreed that natural law property authorizes the sovereign[26] to take life in order to vindicate justice. Only Jeremy Bentham[27] was ambivalent[28]. Washington, Jefferson, and Franklin endorsed it. Abraham Lincoln authorized executions for deserters[29] in wartime. Alexis de Tocqueville[30], who expressed profound[31] respect for American institutions, believed that the death penalty was indispensable to the support of social order. The United States Constitution, widely admired as one of the seminal[32] achievements in the history of humanity, condemns cruel and inhuman punishment, but does not condemn capital punishment.

**7** Should the state have the power to take away people's lives?

13. (7) The death penalty is state-sanctioned murder. This is the defense with which Messrs. Willie and Shaw hoped to soften the resolve of those who sentenced them to death. By saying in effect, "You're not better than I am," the murderer seeks to bring his accusers down to his own level. It is also a popular argument among opponents of capital punishments, but a transparently false one. Simply put, the state has rights that the private individual does not. In a democracy, those rights are given to the state by the electorate[33]. The execution of a lawfully condemned killer is no more an act of murder than is legal imprisonment an act of kidnapping. If an individual forces a neighbor to pay him money under threat of punishment, it's called extortion[34]. If the state does it, it's called taxation. Rights and responsibilities surrendered by the individual are what give the state its power to govern. This contract is the foundation of civilization itself.

14. Everyone wants his or her rights, and will defend them jealously. Not everyone, however, wants responsibility, especially the painful responsibility that come with law enforcement. Twenty-one years ago a woman named Kitty Genovese was assaulted[35] and murdered on a street in New York. Dozens of neighbors heard her cries for help but did nothing to assist her. They didn't even call the police. In such a climate the criminal understandably grows bolder. In the presence of moral cowardice, he lectures us on our supposed failings and tries to equate his crimes with our quest for justice.

15. The death of anyone—even a convicted killer—diminishes us all. But we are diminished even more by a justice system that fails to function. It is an illusion to let ourselves believe that doing away with capital punishment removes the murderer's deed from our conscience. The rights of society are paramount[36]. When we protect guilty lives, we give up innocent lives in exchange. When opponents of capital punishment say to the state: "I will not let you kill in my name," they are also saying to murderers: "You can kill in your own name as long as I have an excuse for not getting involved."

16. It is hard to imagine anything worse than being murdered while neighbors do nothing. But something worse exists. When those same neighbors shrink back from justly punishing the murderer, the victim dies twice.

## Notes

1. clemency /'klemənsi/ *n.*   kindness when giving a punishment
2. aggravated /'ægrəveitid/ *a.*   (of an offence) made more serious by related circumstances
3. mutilate /'mju:tileit/ *v.*   seriously damage (esp a person's body) by removing a part
4. reverence /'revərəns/ *n.*   deep respect
5. burglarize /'bə:gləraiz/ *v.*   break into a building and steal from (it or the people in it)
6. heinous /'heinəs/ *a.*   very shameful, shocking and wicked
7. reprehensible /repri'hensəbl/ *a.*   deserving condemnation
8. lingering /'liŋgəriŋ/ *a.*   slow to reach an end
9. gallows /'gæləuz/ *n.*   a structure consisting of two uprights and a crosspiece, used for hanging a person; execution by hanging
10. lethal /'li:θəl/ *a.*   causing to death
11. chemotherapy /ki:məu'θerəpi/ *n.*   the treatment of diseases using chemicals
12. flagrant /'fleigrənt/ *a.*   (of a bad action, situation, person, etc.) shocking because of being so obvious
13. homicide /'hɔmisaid/ *n.*   an act of murder
14. sentimentality /sentimen'tæliti/ *n.*   tendency to have feelings of tenderness, sadness, or nostalgia
15. strangle /'stræŋgl/ *v.*   kill by pressing on the throat with the hands, a rope, etc to stop breathing
16. status /steitəs/ *n.*   a written law passed by a legislative body; a rule of an organization or institution

17. penitentiary /ˈpeniˈtenʃəri/ *n.* (in North America) a prison for people convicted of serious crimes
18. sophistic /səˈfistik/ *a.* apparently sound but really fallacious
19. proscribe /prəuˈskraib/ *v.* forbid, esp. by law
20. Immanuel Kant (1724—1804) German philosopher, one of the foremost thinkers of the Enlightenment
21. John Locke (1632—1704): English philosopher. He is considered the founding figure of British empiricism
22. Thomas Hobbes (1588—1679) English philosopher and political theorist
23. Jean-Jacques Rousseau (1712—1778) Swiss-French philosopher
24. Baron de Montesquieu (1689—1755): French philosopher and satirist
25. James Mill (1773—1836) Scottish philosopher, historian, and economist
26. sovereign /ˈsɔvrin/ *a.* One that exercises supreme authority within a limited sphere; a king or queen who is the supreme ruler of a country
27. Jeremy Bentham (1748—1832) British moral philosopher and legal theorist, the earliest expounder of utilitarianism
28. ambivalent /æmˈbivələnt/ *a.* having mixed feelings or contradictory ideas about sth or sb
29. deserter /diˈzə:tə/ *n.* a member of the armed forces who deserts
30. Alexis de Tocqueville French political scientist, historian, and politician
31. profound /prəˈfaund/ *a.* very great or intense; showing great knowledge or insight; demanding deep study or thought
32. seminal /ˈseminəl/ *a.* (of a work, event, or idea) strongly influencing later developments
33. electorate /iˈlektəreit/ *n.* the body of people in a country or area who are entitled to vote in an election
34. extortion /ikˈstɔ:ʃən/ *n.* the act of obtaining by force, threats, or other unfair means
35. assault /əˈsɔ:lt/ *v.* attack violently; rape
36. paramount /ˈpærəmaunt/ *a.* more important than anything else; supreme; having supreme power

## A Critical Reader (II)

In your opinion, is it the right time to abolish the death penalty in China now? Why or why not?

# A Critical Writer

## I. Basic Writing Techniques

### 1. Style and word choice

**1.1** This is an argumentative essay. In this type of essay, the author often weighs the two sides of a controversial issue, takes a firm stand and tries to persuade the reader to take his/her position. The style of this article is standard. Please read the following example.

e.g.

Life is indeed **precious**, and I believe the death penalty helps to **affirm** this fact. Had the death penalty been a real possibility in the minds of these murderers (**an inverted sentence in subjunctive mood**), they might well have stayed their hand. (Paragraph 3)

Please find two more examples from the article.

**1.2** It is important that opinions are presented clearly and strongly in argumentative essays; therefore, words that can convey the authors' opinion and attitude are often used to achieve this purpose. Please read the following example. Pay attention to the words in bold face.

e.g.

1) It is a **curiosity** of modern life that we find ourselves being **lectured** on morality by **cold-blooded** killers. (Paragraph 2)

2) In such a climate the criminal **understandably** grows **bolder**. In the presence of moral **cowardice**, he lectures us on our **supposed failings** and tries to equate his crimes with our quest for justice. (Paragraph 14)

Please locate two more examples from the article.

### 2. Basic rules for good sentences and paragraphs

**2.1** Please read Paragraph 10 again and appreciate its conciseness, unity and coherence.

1) Conciseness: no redundant words.

Compare the following two sentences and consider how conciseness is achieved in sentence b.

(1) Mr. Shaw committed two murders, for which he was given the death penalty sentence. In fact, he admitted that one week before these murders, he killed a 14-year-old girl and cut her body into pieces.

(2) Mr. Shaw committed another murder a week before the two for which he was executed, and admitted

2) Unity in a paragraph:

What functions does the first sentence serve? How do the other sentences relate to the main idea of this paragraph?

3) Coherence:

In Paragraph 10, how do each sentence and the whole paragraph achieve coherence?

**Analysis**

Paragraph 10 is a good example of conciseness, unity and coherence. There are not redundant words in this paragraph. Sentence 1: Capital punishment <u>cheapens the value of human life</u>.

The first sentence presents the opinion on the other side.

Sentence 2: On the contrary, it can be easily demonstrated that <u>death penalty strengthens the value of human life</u>.

Sentence 2 presents the counter argument, which is the author's opinion.

Sentence 3: <u>If the penalty for rape were lowered, clearly it would signal a lessened regard for the victims' suffering, humiliation, and personal integrity.</u>

Sentence 4: <u>It would cheapen their horrible experience, and expose them to an increase danger of recurrence.</u>

Sentence 5: <u>When we lower the penalty for murder, it signals a lessened regard for the values of the victim's life.</u>

Sentences 3, 4, 5, refute the opposite opinion by relating the serious consequences that would result if the death penalty is abolished , thus emphasizes the point that the death penalty serves the exact function of paying due respect to human life and hence successfully retorts the opposite opinion. In terms of structure, sentence 3 summarizes the authors' opinion and sentences 4 and 5 illustrate in more detail. The three sentences are logically connected and well unified under the same central idea.

Sentence 6: Some critics of capital punishment, such as columnist Jimmy Breslin, have suggested that <u>a life sentence is actually a harsher penalty for murder than death</u>.

Sentence 7: This is <u>sophistic nonsense</u>.

Sentence 8: A few killers may decide not to appeal a death sentence, but <u>the overwhelming majority make every effort to stay alive</u>.

Sentence 6 presents an argument for the opposite side and sentences 7 and 8 retort it.

Sentence 9: <u>It is by exacting the highest penalty for the taking of human life that we affirm the highest value of human life.</u>

Sentence 9 reiterates the author's position using the structure "it is … that" to emphasizes it and thus persuasively closes the paragraph.

The whole paragraph is unified under one central idea. The sentences are logically connected and cohesive devices such as the transitional phrase "on the contrary", the pronoun "it", and the conjunction "but" are used to help the ideas flow naturally from one to another, forming one coherent paragraph.

**2.2 Imitation**

Translate the Chinese sentences into English by simulating the structure of the given English sentences.

1) One does not have to like the death penalty in order to support it any more

than one must like radical surgery, radiation, or chemotherapy in order to find necessary these attempts at curing cancer. (Paragraph 6)

我们没有必要为了制止谋杀而把法律上认定的杀人犯（其中一些可能无辜）统统杀掉，正如我们不能为了避免交通事故而销毁所有我们认为有严重故障的车辆一样。

_____

_____

2) The execution of a lawfully condemned killer is no more an act of murder than is legal imprisonment an act of kidnapping. (Paragraph 13)

保护杀人犯，让其免于受罚的行为无异于纵容犯罪。

_____

_____

**2.3** Arrange the following sentences in the best order to create the best paragraph. Find the one sentence that does not belong because it is irrelevant. Pay attention to the logical connection between ideas.

_____ One-fourth of those exonerated of murder had received a death sentence, while half of those who had been wrongfully convicted of rape or murder faced death or a life behind bars.

_____ For those who have placed unequivocal faith in the US criminal justice system and believe that all condemned prisoners are guilty of the crime of which they were convicted, the data must make for a rude awakening.

_____ Of these, 885 have profiles developed for the registry's website, exonerationregistry.org.

_____ The US criminal justice system is a broken machine that wrongfully convicts innocent people, sentencing thousands of people to prison or to death for the crimes of others, as a new study reveals.

_____ In 2012, the American death penalty has reached a crossroads.

_____ The leading causes of wrongful convictions include perjury, flawed eyewitness identification and prosecutorial misconduct.

_____ Ten of the inmates went to their grave before their names were cleared.

_____ The University of Michigan law school and Northwestern University have compiled a new National Registry of Exonerations—a database of over 2,000 prisoners exonerated between 1989 and the present day, when DNA evidence has been widely used to clear the names of innocent people convicted of rape and murder.

### 3. Basic rule for good essays: Well-organized structure

#### 3.1 Questions

1) Please identify the introduction, body and conclusion part of this article. Give a brief description of what the author presents in each part.

2) How are the paragraphs in the body part of the article organized? Can their position be changed?

### 3.2 Analysis

This essay has very clear structure. Paragraphs 1—4 constitute the introduction section of this article. The author uses two cases to introduce the topic and presents the thesis at the end of the introduction: the death penalty should not be abolished. In the body paragraphs (Paragraphs 5—13), the author refutes the arguments on the opposite side one by one, using numbers to organize them. For each point, he provides sufficient and compelling evidence to support his point. The last three paragraphs (Paragraphs 14—16) form the conclusion part, in which the author reiterates his point and concludes the discussion. The article has clear central idea that guides the discussion. The logical flow is smooth. Cohesive devices such as transitions, pronouns, key words, etc. are used to help achieve coherence of the article.

### 3.3 Working out an outline

Do you think it is the right time for China to abolish the death penalty? At the end of this section, you will be asked to write an article on this topic. Now, think carefully about this topic and write a working outline of your essay. Make sure you include your thesis, topic sentences and brief descriptions of what you plan to do to describe each paragraph.

## II. Specific Writing Techniques

### 1. Argumentative essay

An argumentative essay not only gives information but also present an argument with the PROS (supporting ideas) and CONS (opposing ideas) of a controversial issue. The author should clearly take a stand and try to persuade an opposing audience to agree with his/her point of view. The primary objective is to persuade people to change beliefs that many of them do not want to change.

The introduction of an argumentative essay usually consists of four parts:
1) Introduces the topic
2) Explains the importance of the issue
3) States there is an opposite side on it
4) Presents the thesis of the article and describes how the article is going to be structured.

In an argumentative essay it is important to find powerful and strong evidence to support your point; it is also important to refute the opposing arguments, so as to prove your position is more valid and convince others to agree with you. These two elements can be dealt with in separate sections in an argumentative essay. The author can first argue for his/her position, usually in several paragraphs and in the next section, usually in one or two paragraphs, refute the opposing arguments. In such structure, the focus is on arguing for the author's position. There is another pattern of organization, the above two elements are combined into one section; that is, the author focuses on refuting the opposite arguments, thereby proves that the opponents are wrong or their position is inferior. Text A is a good example of such structure.

However, no matter which pattern is adopted to organize the essay, it needs to be pointed out, if the opponents have some valid points, the author should acknowledge them before proceeding to argue for his/her points. This will demonstrate that the author is fair and make his/her arguments more persuasive.

**2. Read the introduction section of Text A and identify the four parts of it.**

**3. Read Paragraph 7 and analyze how the author refutes the argument on the opposite side.**

**4. Write a paragraph arguing against the opinion presented in the following topic sentence. Make sure you use concrete evidence to support your opinion.**

After being in prison for some time and receiving proper education, convicted murderers generally repent what they have done and often try to make compensations for the damages they have caused the society or the victims' family.

## III. Your Turn to Write an Essay

Do you think it is the right time for China to abolish the death penalty? Please write an essay on this topic. Choose one of the patterns of organization introduced in this section.

### Pearls of Wisdom

1. For centuries the death penalty, often accompanied by barbarous refinements, has been trying to hold crime in check; yet crime persists.
—Albert Camus

2. I don't think you should support the death penalty to seek revenge. I don't think that's right. I think the reason to support the death penalty is because it saves other people's lives. — George W. Bush

3. Do not be too eager to deal out death in judgment. For even the very wise cannot see all ends. —J. R. R. Tolkien

4. It's just really tragic after all the horrors of the last 1,000 years we can't leave behind something as primitive as government sponsored execution.
—Russ Feingold

5. If we are to abolish the death penalty, I should like to see the first step taken by my friends—the murderers. —Alphonse Karr

6. "I cannot stand the thought of being responsible for someone being falsely accused and facing the death penalty. For me this is a moral issue...I don't want to be part of a system that sends innocent people...to the death penalty." —Sen. Edith Prague

7. "For me, the most compelling reason to reject the death penalty is to set ourselves on the path to the kind of society we really want for our future. I want something better for our future. We cannot confront darkness with darkness and expect light."
—Sen. Gayle Slossberg, D-Miford

# Text C

## People Should Choose When to Retire

By Patrick Mattimore

**A Critical Reader**

1. Opinions are flying about a looming economic problem as April's census data revealed that people above the age of 60 now account for 13.3% of China's total population and the number is still rising. Commentators have made many good suggestions to address the problem including improving the social security and pension systems, building more nursing home facilities, and developing new population policies with the older demographic[1] in mind.

2. However, the elephant in the room not being addressed is the outdated mandatory[2] retirement policy. In China, the mandatory retirement age is 60 for men and 55 for women. The policy is intended to create employment opportunities for younger workers but leaves large numbers of otherwise productive and healthy people unemployed and unproductive. There is also a large body of behavioral research which suggests that workers prefer flexible retirement policies and that such policies would psychologically benefit those workers.

3. From a societal viewpoint, mandatory retirement—especially at the youthful ages of 60 and 55 respectively—makes little sense. Capable individuals forced to retire become net expenses rather than economic contributors. As life spans increase, society can ill afford to put people on the dole for sustained periods. <u>Whatever benefits society realizes from employing more young workers will be outweighed by the costs of supporting older unemployed persons.</u>

[1] Do you think a mandatory retirement policy will have a positive or negative effect on the society? Why?

[2] What is the thesis of this article?

4. There is also evidence that foreclosing choice may be harmful. The effects of choice and enhanced personal responsibility for the aged were the subject of a famous field experiment conducted by Yale Professor Judith Rodin and Harvard Psychologist Ellen Langer in the 1970s. The researchers studied the effects of enhanced personal responsibility and choice on 91 nursing home residents. Residents who were in the experimental group (choice) were given a communication emphasizing their responsibility for themselves, whereas the communication given to a 2nd group (cared for) stressed the staff's responsibility for them. The latter message of dependency is essentially what we communicate unconsciously to people when they are forced to retire.

5. In the Langer/Rodin study the choice group was, for example, given responsibility for taking care of a plant and allowed to choose movie nights, whereas the cared for group did not have the plant responsibility or movie night choice. Seventy-one percent of the cared for group got worse in only 3 weeks. The health of the residents encouraged to make decisions for themselves actually improved. They were more active and happier. They were more mentally alert. When the researchers returned 18 months later, twice as many residents in the choice group were still alive.

6. These findings fit in well with the work on learned helplessness in dogs which psychologist Martin Seligman did in the late 1960s, and on Langer and Rodin's own studies on the perception of control.

7. Learned helplessness theory is the view that clinical depression and related mental illnesses may result from a perceived absence of control over the outcome of a situation.

8. By forcibly taking away persons' abilities to choose when to retire and placing them into dependent roles, society may be unintentionally accelerating mental and physical problems of the aged and creating an even larger drain[3] on the country's financial resources.

*(Patrick Mattimore is a 60-year-old former psychology teacher living and working in Beijing.)*

3 How is the idea presented in Paragraph 4 supported in Paragraph 5?

4 What are the author's arguments against a mandatory retirement policy?

5 What evidences does the author use to support his arguments?

> **Notes**
>
> 1. demographic /ˌdeməˈgræfik/ n.   in business, a demographic is a group of people in a society, especially people in a particular age group. (BUSINESS)
> 2. mandatory /ˈmændətəri/ a.   required or commanded by authority; obligatory
> 3. drain /dreɪn/ n.   a gradual outflow or loss; consumption or depletion

## A Critical Reader (II)

1. In your opinion, is it feasible to abolish the mandatory retirement policy now? Why or why not?
2. Based on what you learn from this article, what suggestions can you give the retired people to enrich their life so as to prevent psychological problems they might encounter?

## A Critical Writer

### I. Basic Writing Techniques

**1. Style and word choice**

**Consider the following questions:**

1) Think about the four levels of diction described in the introduction section of this book. What kind of writing style does the author follow (formal vs. informal)? Which level of diction does this article adopt?

2) How is the writing style reflected through the word choice and sentence structure? Support your opinion by locating from the article ten examples of word choice that are consistent with the writing style.

e.g.

(1) The policy is **intended to** create employment opportunities for younger workers but leaves large numbers of **otherwise productive** and healthy people unemployed and unproductive. (Paragraph 2)

(2) **Capable** individuals forced to retire become net expenses rather than **economic contributors**. (Paragraph 3)

(3) By forcibly taking away persons' abilities to choose when to retire and placing them into dependent roles, society may be unintentionally **accelerating** mental and physical problems of the aged and creating an even larger **drain** on the country's **financial resources**. (Paragraph 8)

## 2. Basic Rules for Good Sentences and paragraphs

**2.1** Please read Paragraph 5 and analyze how it is developed, how unity, coherence are achieved and what transitional devices are used.

**2.2 Analysis**

1) Unity:

This paragraph displays good unity. The whole paragraph focuses on the Langer/Rodin study. It describes the research procedure and the research results, providing relevant statistics as support. The paragraph is tightly united under the central idea. No irrelevant details could be identified.

2) Coherence and Transition:

The coherence of this paragraph is accomplished by logically presenting the research procedure of a study, and using some effective cohesive devices to indicate the connections between ideas presented in the sentences. The cohesive devices used include: **conjunctive adverb** "whereas", the **transitional phrase** "for example" the pronoun "they" and phrases such as "eighteen months later".

## 3. Basic Rules for Good Essays: Well-organized Structure

**3.1** Please make an outline of the article and discuss how unity and coherence is achieved in this article.

**3.2** Paragraph 3 and 4 both argue against mandatory retirement policy. How are they different?

**3.3 Analysis**

This essay is well-organized, with a clear structure.

**Part one (Paragraph 1 and 2):** the lead-in

1) **Paragraph 1 and 2** is the introduction section of the article. The author introduces the topic with some convincing statistics and facts. At the end of Paragraph 2, the author presents the thesis.

**Part two (Paragraph 3—7):** the development

2) **Paragraph 3** discusses the drawbacks of the mandatory retirement system from a societal point of view, providing logical support for the thesis.

3) **Paragraph 4 to 7** provides statistical support by describing a study on retired people and discusses how it supports the author's view.

**Part three (Paragraph 8):** the end-conclusion

4) In **Paragraph 8**, the author summarizes the main idea and concludes the essay.

## II. Special Writing Techniques

1. Compare the following two paragraphs. How are they different in terms of their writing style? What factors might have caused the differences? Share your ideas with a partner.

1) Retirement is the point where a person stops employment completely. A person may also semi-retire by reducing work hours. Many people choose to retire when they are eligible for private or public <u>pension</u> benefits, although some are forced to retire when physical conditions no longer allow the person to work anymore (by illness or accident) or as a result of legislation concerning their position. (http://en.wikipedia.org/wiki/Retirement)

2) Why do we retire early? We were on a fast track, hamster wheel of life, and made the decision to retire early to pursue traveling and other interests. Many older retired folks told us "do it now, while you're young". We heard them and took their advice. Life isn't a game where whoever has the most money or stuff, biggest house, or newest car wins. We assessed ourselves, created this opportunity, and went for it.

(http://www.retireearlylifestyle.com/20questions.htm)

**Analysis:** The first paragraph is a serious piece of writing, written for an encyclopedia, with the purpose to inform or educate. Its audience is generally assumed to be educated and it is supposed to disseminate sound, reliable information. Therefore the style and word choice of this paragraph are standard and the tone is serious. In contrast, the second paragraph is from a couple's website. The purpose of this paragraph is to share the experiences of their retired life with others. The audience could be anyone who is interested in their life, and hence the authors are treating the audiences as if they were their friends or acquaintances. For this reason, the writing adopts an informal style and the tone is personal, casual, friendly and entertaining. The style and word choice of both paragraphs are appropriate for their purpose and audience.

2. Features of Academic Writing

2.1 **Academic writing refers to writing for academic purposes such as: research papers, theses, dissertations, technical reports etc.**

**Objective, Style, and Tone**

The objective of an academic essay is to inform rather than entertain. Its purpose is often to disseminate reliable knowledge to a critical and educated audience. Therefore, it often adopts a serious, impersonal tone, a standard style, an objective stance and accurate diction. To be specific, an academic essay frequently uses:

- the passive voice but overuse of passive voice is not advisable
- the third person rather than the first person ( it rather than I or we)
- things rather than people as subjects of sentences.

**Organization**

Academic writing in English has a linear, straightforward structure. An academic essay clearly presents a main theme (thesis), usually in the introduction section and develops the thesis in the rest of the essay by providing effective support for it. In other words, the main line of argument is followed all through the essay, without digressions or repetitions.

**Word and Sentence Complexity**

Academic writing as a form of written language generally has higher level of complexity than spoken language in terms of word choice and sentence structure. For example, it uses longer and more complex words, more noun-based phrases than verb-based phrases. In addition, academic writing often has more grammatical complexity and larger variety in sentence structure, which can be exemplified by its frequent use of subordinate clauses and passives.

**2.2 If you are asked to retire at the age stipulated by Chinese law, will you feel happy about it? Why or why not? Explain your reasons in one paragraph. Notice: your paragraph should have two versions, each addressing a different audience. Make sure you adjust the style and tone of your writing to accommodate your audience.**

Version 1: This paragraph will be part of a letter you write to your parents.

_____
_____
_____
_____
_____

Version 2: This paragraph will be part of an essay you turn in to your college professor.

_____
_____
_____
_____
_____

## III. Your Turn to Write an Essay

In your opinion, is it the right time for China to abolish mandatory retirement policy? Why or why not? Write an essay on this topic. Make sure your essay has effective support and appropriate style and tone.

## Pearls of Wisdom

1. Retirement: It's nice to get out of the rat race, but you have to learn to get along with less cheese. —Gene Perret

2. Retire from work but not from life. —M. K. Soni

3. Retirement has been a discovery of beauty for me. I never had the time before to notice the beauty of my grandkids, my wife, the tree outside my very own front door. And, the beauty of time itself. —Hartman Jule

4. The key to retirement is to find joy in the little things. —Susan Miller

5. Retirement is the beginning of life, not the end. —the American international bestseller —How to Retire Happy, Wild, and Free

6. Retirement is like a long vacation in Las Vegas. The goal is to enjoy it the fullest, but not so fully that you run out of money. —Jonathan Clements

7. Retirement is a time to make the inner journey and come face to face with your flaws, failures, prejudices, and all the factors that generate thoughts of unhappiness. Retirement is not a time to sleep, but a time to awaken to the beauty of the world around you and the joy that comes when you cast out all the negative elements that cause confusion and turmoil in your mind and allow serenity to prevail. —Howard Salzman

8. Don't think of retiring from the world until the world will be sorry that you retire. —Samuel Johnson

# Corpus-based Exercises (10)

## I. Key Word: society

**1.** In this chapter, we talk about controversial issues in *society*. How is the word *society* used in context? What adjectives often precede it? Read the following concordance lines and try to make your analysis.

| | | |
|---|---|---|
| Poland is a group-oriented | society | , which means that cooperation is strongly |
| even in our disintegrating | society | we obey them . |
| has hardly disappeared from modern | society | — even the U . S . |
| But America became a wealthy | society | through work , work and more work . |
| A commonly accepted rule of civilized | society | is that when   public health is     5 |
| It results in an often angry , chaotic | society | , where every trivial act is interpreted as |
| as an envoy from the Royal | society | , and this led to my staying there |

| | | |
|---|---|---|
| the establishment of a great industrial | **society** | , but there was the other side |
| but because it is right . If a free | **society** | cannot help the many who are poor , it |
| In a democratic | **society** | this means that the public needs to          10 |
| intelligent members of | **society** | Some teachers argue that calculators |
| Self-Reliance in a technological | **society** | my 15 students read Emerson, Thoreau , |
| India had gone from an agricultural | **society** | to the cyber-revolution , without passing |
| now as required an attitude in polite | **society** | as is , say , belief in democracy or |
| as a multiracial and multicultural | **society** | This is absolutely new .There is no          15 |
| In an increasingly competitive | **society** | , life will become tougher for people |
| that have spread throughout American | **society** | must be fought . |
| If you go to an aboriginal | **society** | living in the forest they don't use locks , |
| young Jack to civilized upper-class | **society** | , horrifying her mother and making her |
| entered the new century , human | **society** | is beginning its move from          20 |

The following list of collocations of the word *society* is drawn from the above concordance lines.

| | | |
|---|---|---|
| aboriginal society | group-oriented society | polite society |
| agricultural society | human society | royal society |
| chaotic society | increasingly competitive society | technological society |
| civilized society | industrial society | upper-class society |
| democratic society | modern society | wealthy society |
| disintegrating society | modern society | |
| free society | multicultural society | |

**2. Fill in the blanks of the following sentences with the phrases listed above.**

1) In a _____, the basic needs are met with little difficulty. Food and shelter is readily available and easily accessible to the majority of people.

2) A _____ is a society , Group, school or organization where people of different races, cultures and religions live, work and communicate with each other in peace.

3) "Women and men are competing all the time and we live in an _____, whether that's competing with status symbols, partner choice, commercial or academic success, or looks," says clinical psychologist Joanne Corrigan.

4) An ordered society is one with rules and consequences for breaking those rules. A _____ is freer, without order or law, and without consequences.

5) The right to freedom of speech as one of the basic human rights is enshrined in main international human rights documents. Freedom of speech (synonym Freedom of expression) is the inseparable element of a _____.

## II. Key Words : argue and argument

1. In this chapter, we discuss how you can present your *arguments* effectively, but do you know how the words *argue* and *argument* are used? Study the following concordance lines and complete the exercises that follow.

| | | |
|---|---|---|
| Others | **argue** | that the rise could be due to |
| We live in a time when we | **argue** | about pragmatism and compromises in our quest |
| because many psychologists | **argue** | that IAD is not an actual mental health disorder . |
| and never did he | **argue** | with his wife or defy her wishes . |
| chief executives regularly | **argue** | in their annual reports that    5 |
| If you 're going to start trying to | **argue** | about who deserves to live more than the next one |
| He even has to | **argue** | with the teacher , once he understands what the |
| Many experts | **argue** | for and against this new move in the economy . |
| Only an anarchist would | **argue** | for complete government deregulation of |
| We will | **argue** | over it and may even , as a nation , make some    10 |
| or yourself without starting an | **argument** | . I call these techniques " Tongue Fu ! " |
| One effective way to avoid an | **argument** | is to say , " We 're both right ! " and move on to a |
| discussion is turning into an | **argument** | . Just because you aren't seeing eye to eye doesn't |
| But the most important | **argument** | for a broad education is that in studying the |
| who cut through | **argument** | , debate and doubt to offer a solution everybody    5 |
| Gingrich dismissed the | **argument** | that those who benefit from affirmative action , |
| terrorism , offers a compelling | **argument** | for pursuing a global digital monetary system. |
| Every holiday there is a serious | **argument** | in the family about whether to visit your parents or |
| or adopting a child ) is not an | **argument** | for denying them the right to clone . Or consider an |
| is much more than an | **argument** | against the latest racially biased theory .    10 |
| step by step through an | **argument** | encouraging him or her to explore ideas |
| seem to give support to the | **argument** | that outstanding mental abilities are largely the |
| one day in the midst of an | **argument** | " Well , Sam , " I replied , " |

2. Extract the following types of collocations of the words *argue* or *argument*:
argue + prepositions   verb + argument   adjective + argument

_____   _____   _____
_____   _____   _____
_____   _____   _____
_____   _____   _____
_____   _____   _____
_____   _____   _____

# Appendix — Practical Writing Samples

## I. Notes

Note is in essence an informal letter adopted in such various occasions as invitation, congratulation, sympathy, request, and etc., which is not posted and mailed to the recipient, but delivered to the addressee care of someone, positioned on the desk or even pasted on the door. Since in most occasions the relationship between the addressor and addressee is close and intimate, the language employed is usually simple, direct and even sometimes colloquial, and the format is not so rigid as the formal posted letter.

In general, a note consists of five essential components, time, salutation, body, complimentary close and signature. In terms of time, the American way of expression is always favored—start with month, followed by date and ended with year, but year could be omitted for the timeliness is one of key features of notes. And the salutation mainly rests in the relationship of sender with the receiver, distant or close, familiar or estranged, where the close friends and relatives are directly addressed by their first name, but the nodding acquaintances, elders or seniors are saluted by the their last name with a suitable title, courteous (Mr., Mrs., Miss, Ms.) or professional (Professor, Doctor, Director), placed before the last name. As for the body of note, it's more appropriate to adopt the indentation instead of the block usually with the first line of the first paragraph indented by four or five letters. Finally, the complimentary should correspond with the salutation with regard to the relationship, which therefore varies from such casual expressions as "Yours", "Yours always", "(with) Love", to the extremely formal wording like "Respectfully yours", "Obediently yours" (which denotes the distant relationship and always the subjection of sender to the recipient in point of age or social status ), but between these two ends, several other expressions are more flexible to fit into different situations, such as "Yours sincerely", "Truthfully yours", "Yours cordially", "Faithfully yours".

### 1. Asking for Leave

April 14, 2009

Dear Mr. Foster,

    I am asking for one week's leave of absence from the 15th to 25th, both days inclusive, in order to return to see my mother, who is now seriously ill. To support my request, I have attached a telegram received from my father. I will be very appreciative if you will grant my request, and I will do my best to make up any lessons I miss during my absence.

Yours respectfully,<br>Sophie

## 2. Invitation

Nov. 7, 2011<br>Nov. 7

Dear Mark,

  The UESTC English Drama Festival will start on the evening of November 11th at the UESTC auditorium on the new campus, and we would like to invite you to attend the opening ceremony. The Festival is hosted by the Department of Foreign Languages and the students you taught last year will put on Act II of Hamlet during the opening ceremony. We are all looking forward to meeting you again and hope you will enjoy the play. Details of the schedule will be mailed to you later.

Sincerely yours,<br>Sophie

## 3. Reply to an Invitation

Nov. 8

Dear Sophie,

  I am very appreciative of your kind invitation to the Drama Festival. However, I won't be able to attend because I must travel to Beijing for an International academic conference this Friday and will not return until next Monday. What a shame that I should miss such a significant occasion!

  I send you my best wishes for the complete success of your annual feast!

Yours sincerely,<br>Mark

## 4. Sympathy and Consolation

Nov. 14, 2011

Dear Sara,

    I'm very sorry to hear about your being beaten by the security guard at Seven and Twelve. I simply can't imagine how they could allow such a thing to happen. I'll pray for your speedy recovery and hope to see you soon on the campus. By the way, the guard is detained in custody now and the shop has also been deplored by the press and the public for its loose management. Take care and best regards, and my heart is with you,

Yours always,<br>Sue

---

May 5, 2009

Dear Mildred,

    I am greatly saddened by the news of the passing of your Aunt Mabel. I know how difficult this must be for you. My thoughts are with you during this difficult time. What encouraging words she used to give us! Aunt Mabel was such a kind and gentle soul. Her great humor, warm hospitality, eagerness to help, and, above all, her willingness to listen to us will forever be remembered. Please accept our profoundest condolences.

Yours,<br>Amy

## 5. Complaints

Nov. 27, 2011

Dear Manager,

    I would like to air my complaints about the very poor service that I received at your restaurant on the 25th of November. The staff displayed a large amount of incompetence and a bad attitude towards customers. No one attended to me for about ten minutes, and when the waiter finally showed up, he showed a severe lack of interest. He had to take my order three times, but even so, he still brought me the wrong food!

    I demand that the staff in your restaurant improve their own work ethic and service quality in order to better cater to the perspective customers.

Yours sincerely,<br>Sophie

Nov. 15, 2010

Dear Manager,

 I'm a customer of your company, and bought a MP5 last Sunday in your store. Actually, the Mp5 is of high quality which really pleases me, but I'd like to draw your attention to the poor service of the salesman. He showed indifference to me and even shouted at me. This type of customer treatment is intolerable. I would strongly suggest that you retrain your sales staff for the sake of your company. I truly hope that some immediate and effective measures are taken.

Yours sincerely,<br>Elise

## 6. Inquiry and Request

Dec. 5, 2011

Dear Sir or Madame,

 With reference to your advertisement on the West China Metropolitan News, I am writing to consult with you about politics-intensive classes for the national postgraduate entrance examination. I would like to be enrolled in this New Oriental program. Please contact me with more detailed information related to what specific courses will be offered, who will give the lessons and how much I should pay for the entire training. Your prompt response is greatly appreciated.

 Sincerely yours,
 Helen

Dec. 4, 2011

Dear David,

 I am sorry to trouble you, but nobody comes to mind, except you, regarding a problem I have. I wonder if you could possibly lend me 20 Yuan. My debit card of China Construction Bank was accidentally swallowed by the automatic teller machine yesterday and I've run out of cash. It is only temporary because I've reported it to the issuing bank, which promised to handle the matter instantly. I will repay you the moment I retrieve the card. Your timely financial assistance will be gratefully appreciated and remembered.

Yours,<br>Sammy

## 7. IOU and Receipt

Dec. 12, 2011

Borrowed from Sammy the amount of RMB Twenty Yuan (RMB 20) to be repaid within two weeks from this date together with the agreed interest at one percent.

Yours,
David

Dec. 12, 2011

To Sammy,
IOU in the amount of RMB Twenty Yuan (RMB 20) to be paid back within two weeks from this date together with the agreed interest at one percent per week.

Yours,
David

Dec. 12, 2011

To Sammy,
Two weeks from this date I promise to pay Sammy back the sum of RMB Twenty Yuan (RMB 20) at the agreed interest of one percent per week.

Yours,
David

Dec. 26, 2011

Received from Sammy the amount of RMB Twenty Yuan (RMB 20) with the agreed weekly one-percent interest.

Yours,
David

## II. Letter

Letter writing is a time-honored tradition passed down from generation to generation through the present day and will be undoubtedly perpetuated for its functions as a messenger of information, a bridge of interpersonal communication and an emotional bond between people. There exist five principles for English letter writing indispensable to a good and effective letter, that is, consideration (the writer is supposed to shift from his/her own position and perspective to that of the reader by discarding "I/We- Attitude" and further adopting "You- Attitude" so as to shorten the distance and bridge the gulf), conciseness (the writer is expected to voice his opinion by means of concise and brief expression with the redundant words deleted so that the whole letter would favorably impress the potential reader by its pithiness and directness), clarity (the writer is requested to avoid the ambiguous and equivocal expressions so as to dismiss the possibility of misconception and misunderstanding), courtesy (the writer is required to treat the reader with grace and etiquette by the thoughtful choice of polite and euphemistic words) and correctness (the writer should ensure the correctness of the spelling, punctuation and grammar and also of the data quoted materials).

## 1. The Structure of an English Letter

A letter is composed of six essential parts, the letterhead or heading (the address of sender and the date line), the inside address (the address of receiver), the salutation, the body of letter, the complimentary close and the signature. In addition to the abovementioned elements, several other parts are required in different occasions, especially in the business correspondence, the attention line (when the inside address is directed to a firm name and the writer wishes a certain person or specific department to also be aware of the contents of the letter, an attention line should be used), the subject line (the general idea of the letter contend would be briefly presented in several words as a title of an article in order to invite the due attention of the potential reader), the reference number (it is always used in the business communication where the exchanged letters are kept on filed for the future reference), the enclosure (some other items like product catalogue, cheque, photos, brochure which go together with the letter should be indicated at the end of the letter), the carbon copy notation (when the letter is simultaneously sent to more than one person, it shows a courtesy to tell the reader who also receives a carbon copy of the letter), the postscript (it draws addressee's attention, clarifies a point or makes up the necessary information missed in the body of the letter )

The format of the letter is always one of block pattern, indented pattern or modified pattern (or semi-block pattern). In the block pattern, all the parts are placed flush left with two line space between paragraphs. This style is easy to control and practice, so it is much popular with more practitioners especially in America and Canada. The indented pattern is a traditional British practice with the heading usually in the middle or on the right (each succeeding line of the address is indented by 1 to 3 letters) and the date line on the right, 4 or 5 letters indented in the first line of each paragraph in the body of business letter, and the complimentary close on the right. Since it brings great inconvenience in letter writing even with the aid of the computer, it is comparatively rare compared with the block pattern. The modified pattern is the mixed version of both the block and indented styles with the heading, inside address, date, and complimentary address in resemblance to the indented pattern except the each-line progressive indentation within both the heading and the inside address, but with other parts paralleled with the block pattern.

**The Indented Pattern**

    1. Cheng Kung Sports-Wear Export Trading Co. Ltd
    1 Victory Road
    Tainan City 70101
    Taiwan
    PRC

    2. July 3, 2012

    3. Our Ref.: Exp/ CKS/ 091605
    Your Ref.:

    4. Los Angeles Area Chamber of Commerce
    350 S. Bixel Street
    Los Angeles, CA 90017
    U. S. A.

    5. Attn.: Mr. Jerry Roberts

    6. Dear Sirs:

    7. Looking for Customers
    8. We are desirous of expanding our market to your district, we shall much appreciate it if you will introduce to us some of the reliable clients in Los Angeles that are interested in the importation of ready-made garments.

    We have been exporting ready-made garments which are fashion-designed for more than twenty-five years, and are confident to give our customers the fullest satisfaction. As for our credit standing, please refer to the First Commercial Bank, Taipei.

    Any information with which you may favor us will be much appreciated, and we earnestly await your reply.

    9. Sincerely,
      10. **George Wien**
        George Wien
        General Manager

> 11. GW/al
> 12. Encl.: catalogue; export list
> 13. cc: Mr. Mark Hyman, Marketing Manager
> 14. P.S. Please find a stamped and addressed envelope for your reply.

Notes: 1. heading(or letter head)

2. date

3. reference number

4. inside address

5. attention line

6. salutation

7. subject

8. body of the letter

9. complementary closing

10. signature

11. dictation initials (It consists of the signer's initials in capitals followed by a slash or colon and the typist's lowercase initials, this item serves as a reminder of who prepared the letter. )

12. enclosure

13. carbon copy

14. postscript

**The block pattern**

> Dept. of Chemistry
> Southeast China University
> Nanjing,Jiangsu
> P.R. of China
>
> July 3, 2012
>
> Director
> International Programme
> San Diego University
> San Diego, CA 92282-0930
> USA
>
> Dear Professor Brown,

Per your request, enclosed is the first page of the 104 form for Linda Launius who wants to come to China to study. The original is being mailed today. I hope this will help her to process her passport and to arrive at SCU for the beginning of the Fall semester. Thank you for your attention and assistance.

If there is any further information you require, please let us know.

Sincerely yours,
(Signiture)
Long Ren

Enl.: as stated

**Modified Pattern**

1431 Fifth Avenue
Detroit, MI 48955
USA
Tel: 904-545-3104
Email :annanlansky@pcia.net

July 3, 2012

Ms. Connie Kowlowski, Director
American Language Institute
34256 East Rainbow Avenue
Chengdu, Sichuan 610066
PRC

Dear Ms. Kowlowski:

Are you looking for an experienced, energetic, and professional EFL teacher with 5 years of teaching experience in Japan? Do you need someone who has organized her own successful EFL program? Do your students need a teacher that can create and use excellent EFL teaching materials? I will bring these qualities and more to your students.

I set up and managed 21st Century Education in Tokyo during 2000—2011. As a manager and teacher of this private EFL program, I assumed multiple responsibilities that required management skills and individualized instruction techniques. As a result of my efforts, students who came without knowing their ABC's could, within one year, communicate freely with native English speakers. In a short time, my business expanded from 5 student to 50 students, ages 4 to adult. My 21st Century Education Program continues to expand using the curriculum, teaching materials, and teaching methods I developed.

In addition, I have co-authored four children's nursery rhyme books, two conversational books, five storybooks, and three grammar books. These books are being sold to EFL students in Japan, China and Singapore.

From many years of teaching of experience in Japan and the United States, I have developed positive teacher-student relationship skills, including patience and tact.

The enclosed resume also shows that my academic achievements, education, and work experience directly contribute to my understanding of the academic and personal needs of the students in your EFL program. Let me put my energy, experience, and qualifications to work for your students.

I look forward to an opportunity to discuss how my qualifications meet the teaching need s of your EFL program. I can be contacted at annalansky@pcia.net or (904) 545-3104 from 2 p.m. to 9 p.m.

Sincerely yours,<br>
(signature)<br>
Ms. Anna Lansky

Enclosure

## 2. Envelope

There exists a difference in the way how to address the envelope between the Chinese and English-speaking world, which therefore commands special care and attention if the letter carries the mission to cross the national borders and traverse the broad ocean . The items written on the envelope are generally the same – the address, the return address, stamp, but the arrangement and layout of the same items is slightly distinct. In English envelope, the address of the addressee is located in the center or usually on the right a trifle (or the lower right position), the address of the addressor is positioned on the upper left corner, the stamp is just pasted on the top right corner, and the lower left blank space left is always reserved to some special remarks (for instance, "Private", "Confidential", "Registered", "Express", "Ordinary Mail", "Immediate /Urgent", "Printed Matter", "Sample" or etc.)

Similarly, the layout of envelope is also classified as block form and indented form, where the difference merely lies in whether the line of address is flush left or successively indented by one to three letters.

**The Block Form**

```
addressor's full name
addressor's street address                                    stamp
addressor's city/state/ zip code
addressor's country

                           (title) addressee's full name
                           addressee's street address
                           addressee's city/state/ zip code
                           addressee's country

remarks
```

**The Indented Form**

```
addressor's full name
  addressor's street address                                  stamp
    addressor's city/state/ zip code
      addressor's country

                           (title) addressee's full name
                             addressee's street address
                               addressee's city/state/ zip code
                                 addressee's country

remarks
```

## III. Resume

In the job market, the applicants for jobs are likened to the finished products passively waiting for or actively seeking for the buyers, therefore resume is like a piece of advertisement for the products to introduce themselves, present themselves, recommend themselves and sell themselves to the potential purchaser, the prospective employer. Undoubtedly, the resume (of French origin) or Curriculum Vitae (of Latin origin) is a steppingstone to a promising career since it plays a role of enormous importance to bridge the products and customers, the job-seekers and companies. A resume, as a document referred to by the employer for your background and qualification, should comply with two basic principles, that is, be truthful (no deception, no distortion and no exaggeration) and be selective (one page is always the optimal length of the resume, especially for fresh graduates with redundant expressions and unrelated information trimmed away).

Generally, the information that should be covered in a brief resume is personal information, job objective, education, working experience, reference, besides, special skills, honors and awards and hobbies and interests where necessary to impress the potential employer. The different arrangements of these elements, especially the working experience, lead to two basic styles of resume, reverse chronological resume and functional resume. The former starts with the most recent employment and educational diploma and proceeds backward to the past, which is particularly suitable for the fresh graduates with no or short work history, for people whose job experiences closely parallel the positions they are applying for and for those who have not had periods of unemployment time between jobs. And the latter better fit to the seasoned employee of such abundant experience as to sort out the experience under different titles of special abilities and skills, which is sequenced based on importance and relevance.

**Reverse Chronological Resume**

|  | John Smith |
|---|---|
|  | 14 Milltown Road |
|  | Milltown, RI 02176 |
|  | (401)243-3453 |
|  | Email:jsmith@milltown.com |
| **Objective** | To utilize technology skill obtained through previous experience and education, as well as to pursue opportunities for personal growth |
| **Summary of Skills** | • Excellent computer networking skills<br>• Microsoft Office proficiency<br>• Attention to detail<br>• Experienced in research |
| **Work experience** | 2010  Tech: Foundation  Cambridge, MA<br>LAN Administrator<br>• Maintained Network, ensuring security and productivity<br>• Implemented system for receiving and responding to tech support requests<br>• Inventoried and catalogued tech department equipment |

|  | 2008—2009    MA Dept. of Education    Malden, MA |
|---|---|
|  | Tech support Specialist |
|  | • Upgraded computer systems for Y2K, installed patches and updated software |
|  | • Responded to tech support requests, including printer, installation of software and user training |
|  | • Installed computers and accessories for DOE employees |
|  | • Directed computer-ghosting initicative for DOE department staff |
|  | 2007—2008    MA Dept. of Education    Malden, MA |
|  | • Data Entry Specialist |
|  | • Scanned data into the DOE's mainframe to assist in certification for teachers statewide |
|  | • Examined information for consistency |
| **Reference** | Available upon request |

**Functional Resume**

|  | Jeffrey L. Davis<br>E-mail : jldavis@ncsu.edu<br>Address : 456 East Main Street<br>Wilmington N.C. 28403<br>(910)678-1234 |
|---|---|
| **OBJECTIVE** | Seeking middle grades language arts & social teaching positions where I can contribute my instructional, organizational, and classroom management skills. |
| **EDUCATION** | North Carolina State University, Raleigh, N.C.<br>B.S. Middle Grade Education (Language Arts & Social Studies)<br>3.49/4.00 GPA, May 2010 |
| **CERTIFICATION** | NC Teaching License in Middle Grades Language Arts & Social Studies (June 2010)<br>CPR Certification |

| | |
|---|---|
| **TEACHING EXPERIENCE** | **Student Teacher**, Daniels Middle School, Raleigh, N..C. Jan.2010-April 2010<br>• Taught, assisted, and observed 7th grade students in language arts<br>• Planned and prepared daily lesson plans and instructional materials<br>• Instructed 7th grade language arts classes and was solely responsible for three days during cooperating teacher's emergency leave of absence<br>• Adapted and modified instructions to suit learning styles of students<br>• Created a behavior management plan<br>• Attended 7th grade team meetings (The Barracudas), staff meetings, and parents conferences |
| **OTHER EXPERIENCE** | **Camp Counselor**, Camp High Rocks, Cedar Mountain, N.C. Summer 2009<br>• Co-organized instructional sessions on life skills and social activities<br>• Instructed swimming lake & whitewater canoeing, and backpacking<br>• Supervised group of 15 adolescent boys with cabin maintenance |
| **HONORS/ ACTIVITIES** | **Swimming Instructor**, Wilmington YMCA, Wilmington N.C. Summers 2007, 2008<br>• Instructed multiple levels of swimming<br>• Developed daily lesson plan and communicated with parents<br>• Kappa Delta Pi, International Honor Society<br>• Phi Kappa Tau (Social Committee Chair)<br>• Dean List<br>• Intramural Football & Basketball |
| **INTETERSTS** | Swimming, Canoeing, Weight Training, Hiking, and Traveling |

# British English vs. American English

## I. Different Expressions

| British English | American English |
|---|---|
| anticlockwise | counterclockwise |
| autumn | fall |
| (bank) note（纸币） | (bank) bill |
| basin | sink |
| biscuit | cookie |
| car | automobile/auto |
| car park | parking lot |
| chancellor（大学校长） | president |
| current account | checking account |
| curtains | drapes |
| chips | fries |
| cinema | movie theatre |
| drink-driving | drunk-driving |
| dustbin | garbage can |
| garden | yard |
| ground floor | first floor |
| film | movie |
| flat | apartment |
| football | soccer |
| full stop | period |
| handbag | purse |
| holiday | vacation |
| intersection | crossroads |
| jam | jelly |
| jug | pitcher |
| jumper | sweater |

## Appendix II  British English vs. American English

续表

| British English | American English |
|---|---|
| lamp post | street light |
| lift | elevator |
| lorry | truck |
| motorway | freeway |
| office | bureau |
| page | bellboy |
| Pants（内裤） | underwear |
| pavement | sidewalk |
| petrol | gas/gasoline |
| plait | braid |
| plaster | band-aid |
| porridge | oatmeal |
| post code | zip code |
| rubber | eraser |
| rubbish | trash/garbage |
| first floor | second floor |
| shares | stocks |
| spare time | free time |
| sweets | candy |
| tin | can |
| toilet | bathroom |
| torch | flashlight |
| Trousers（长裤） | pants |
| tube | underway |
| washing powder | detergent |
| zip | zipper |
| at the weekend | on the weekends |
| sit (for)/take an exam | take an exam |

## II. Different Spellings

| British English | American English |
|---|---|
| -ise VS -ize ||
| memorise | memorize |
| analyse | analyze |
| globalisation | globalization |
| realise | realize |
| -our VS -or ||
| colour | color |
| favourite | favorite |
| honour | honor |
| labour | labor |
| -re VS -er ||
| centre | center |
| theatre | theater |
| metre | meter |
| others ||
| dialogue | dialog |
| grey | gray |
| manoeuvre | maneuver |
| programme | program |

## III. Naming of school years in British (except Scotland) and American English

| Age range | British English ||| American English ||
|---|---|---|---|---|---|
| | Name | Alternative name | Syllabus | Name | Alternative name |
| 1–4 | Preschool (optional) ||| | |
| | Nursery | Playgroup | Foundation Stage 1 | Day care | Preschool |
| 3–5 | Primary school ||| | |
| | Reception | Infants reception | Foundation Stage 2 | Pre-kindergarten | Pre-K |
| 5–6 | Year 1 | Infants year 1 | Key Stage 1 | Kindergarten | |
| | | | | Elementary school ||
| 6–7 | Year 2 | Infants year 2 | | 1st grade | |

续表

| Age range | British English ||| American English ||
|---|---|---|---|---|---|
| | Name | Alternative name | Syllabus | Name | Alternative name |
| 7–8 | Year 3 | Junior year 3 | Key Stage 2 | 2nd grade | |
| 8–9 | Year 4 | Junior year 4 | | 3rd grade | |
| 9–10 | Year 5 | Junior year 5 | | 4th grade | |
| 10–11 | Year 6 | Junior year 6 | | 5th grade | |
| 11–12 | Secondary school / High School ||| Middle school | Junior high school |
| | Year 7 | First form | Key Stage 3 | 6th grade | |
| 12–13 | Year 8 | Second form | | 7th grade | |
| 13–14 | Year 9 | Third form | | 8th grade | |
| 14–15 | Year 10 | Fourth form | Key Stage 4, GCSE | High school ||
| | | | | 9th grade | Freshman year |
| 15–16 | Year 11 | Fifth form | | 10th grade | Sophomore year |
| 16–17 | Sixth form (currently optional) ||| 11th grade | Junior year |
| | Year 12 | Lower sixth (AS) | Key Stage 5, A level | | |
| 17–18 | Year 13 | Upper sixth (A2) | | 12th grade | Senior year |